START YOUR OWN

Pet

Business

Additional titles in *Entrepreneur's Startup Series*

Start Your Own

Arts and Crafts Business

Automobile Detailing Business

Bar and Club

Bed and Breakfast

Blogging Business

Business on eBay

Cannabis Business

Car Wash

Child-Care Service

Cleaning Service

Clothing Store and More

Coaching Business

Coin-Operated Laundry

College Planning Consultant Business

Construction and Contracting Business

Consulting Business

Day Spa and More

eBusiness

eLearning or Training Business

Etsy Business

Event Planning Business

Executive Recruiting Business

Fashion Accessories Business

Florist Shop and Other Floral Businesses

Food Truck Business

Freelance Writing Business

Freight Brokerage Business

Gift Basket Business and More

Grant-Writing Business

Graphic Design Business

Green Business

Hair Salon and Day Spa

Home Inspection Service

Import/Export Business

Information Marketing Business

Kid-Focused Business

Lawn Care or Landscaping Business

Mail Order Business

Medical Claims Billing Service

Microbrewery, Distillery, or Cidery

Net Services Business

Nonprofit Organization

Online Coupon or Daily Deal Business

Online Education Business

Personal Concierge Service

Personal Training Business

Pet-Sitting Business and More

Photography Business

Podcasting Business

Public Relations Business

Restaurant and More

Retail Business and More

Self-Publishing Business

Seminar Production Business

Senior Services Business

Specialty Food Businesses

Staffing Service

Transportation Service

Travel Hosting Business

Tutoring and Test Prep Business

Vending Business

Virtual Assistant Business

Wedding Consultant Business

Wholesale Distribution Business

Entrepreneur. STARTUP

START YOUR OWN

Pet

Business

SECOND EDITION

YOUR STEP-BY-STEP GUIDE
TO SUCCESS

**THE STAFF OF ENTREPRENEUR MEDIA
AND RICH MINTZER**

Entrepreneur Press®

Entrepreneur Press, Publisher
Cover Design: Andrew Welyczko
Production and Composition: Eliot House Productions

This publication is designed to provide accurate and authoritative information in regard to the
subject matter covered. It is sold with the understanding that the publisher is not engaged in
rendering legal, accounting, or other professional services. If legal advice or other expert assistance
is required, the services of a competent professional person should be sought.

Entrepreneur Press® is a registered trademark of Entrepreneur Media, Inc.

Library of Congress Cataloging-in-Publication Data
Names: Mintzer, Richard, author. | Sandlin, Eileen Figure. Start your own pet business and more. |
    Entrepreneur Media, Inc., author.
Title: Start your own pet business : your step-by-step guide to success / The Staff of Entrepreneur
    Media, Inc. & Rich Mintzer.
Description: 2nd Edition. | Irvine, CA : Entrepreneur Press, [2023] | Revised edition.
Identifiers: LCCN 2022037058 | ISBN 9781599186696 (trade paperback) | ISBN 9781613084250
    (epub)
Subjects: LCSH: Pet industry—Management. | New business enterprises—Management.
Classification: LCC SF414.7 .M566 2023 | DDC 636.088/7—dc22
LC record available at https://lccn.loc.gov/2022037058

Printed in the United States of America

26 25 24 23   10 9 8 7 6 5 4 3 2 1

Contents

Preface . . . . **xiii**

Chapter 1
Your Customers Are Human **1**

Where to Start? 2

Is Anybody Home? 3

Determine Your Demographics 4

Cat Fight or Mutual Grooming? 4

The Odd Dog Out 5

What Do Humans Want? 5

    Reliability 5

    Trust 6

    Confidence 6

    Professionalism 7

    Customer Care 7

Giving Good Customer Service 8

Pest Control 9

Are You Ready? 11

Chapter 2

Putting the Parts of Your Business in Place......... 13

The Name Game 14

Business Setup 14

McPet Sitter?. 16

Pet-Sitting in Clients' Homes. 18

Making the Pet Environment Comfortable 18

Pet Care in Your Own Home. 19

Pet-Sitting as a Side Job. 20

Don't Zone Out 21

Do You Need a Business Plan?. 22

Business Plan Information 22

Executive Summary 23

Industry Overview 23

Your Credentials 23

Operating Overview. 23

Financials. 23

Startup Costs 24

Forms. 24

Client and Pet Profiles 25

Emergency Care 26

Startup and Operating Capital. 32

Obtaining Financing 35

Chapter 3

Basic Services 37

The Real Goal. 38

Feeding 39

Details, Details 39

Multiple Priorities. 40

Water, Water Everywhere 40

Doing Business. 40

Exercise 42

Get the Lowdown 42

Cat Exercise. 42

Laundry Time. 43

Grooming 43

The Environment. 44

Add Services to Your Menu 45

Setting Clear Rates for Your Services 45
So What Do You Charge? 46
Balancing Diverse Clients 46
  Client Type 1: Day Care 46
  Client Type 2: Long-Weekenders 47
  Client Type 3: Business or Extended Vacation Travelers 47
  Finding the Perfect Client Mix 47
  Your Salary Expectations 48
The Numbers Can Tell a Lot 49

Chapter 4
Putting Your Best Paw Forward 51
Building a Customer Base 52
  Finding Customers 52
The Marketing Plan 53
Your Website and Online Marketing 54
  Email Marketing 55
  Collecting Email Addresses 57
  Social Media 57
Printed Marketing Materials 57
  Business Cards 58
  Brochures 59
  Fliers 61
Paid Advertising 61
Well-Timed Press Releases 63
Vehicle Sign 63
Association Memberships 64
Speak! 65
Try Something Different 65

Chapter 5
Useful Credentials 67
Firsthand Experience 68
  Training 69
  Best in Show 69
  Grooming 70
  First Aid Training 70
  Be a Techie 71
  Visit Your Veterinarian 72

Nutrition 72
Pet Sitters International (PSI) 74
Rounding Out Your Resume 74

Chapter 6

Contracts, Insurance, and Legal Matters 75

Contracts. 76
Insurance. 77
Liability Insurance 77
Bonding 77
Disability Insurance 78
Health Insurance. 78
Auto Insurance 79
Legal Issues. 80
Corporate Structure 80
Employees. 80
Independent Contractors 81
Noncompete and Confidentiality Agreements. 81
Workers' Compensation 82
Internal Revenue Service (IRS) Obligations. 82

Chapter 7

Financial Considerations 85

Class Act 86
Cycles of the Financial Moon 86
Keeping the Books. 87
The Checkbook. 87
The Old-Fashioned Way 87
Software 88
Accounting Methods. 88
Making a Statement. 89
Accountants 89
Taxes 90
Auto Expenses 91
Client Invoices and Receipts 91
Payment Options 92
Policies. 93
Collections 93

Paying Yourself 94

Chapter 8

Raining Cats and Dogs 95

Basic Dog Care 96

    Feeding 96

    Water 97

    Treats 98

    Toys 98

    Dog Restraint 98

Vital Signs 99

    Temperature 99

    Pulse 100

    Respiration 101

    Capillary Refill Time 101

Basic Cat Care 101

    Cat Restraint 101

Allergies 103

Basic First Aid 103

    Signs of Illness 103

    Wound Care 105

    Client Attitude 105

Chapter 9

Other Common House Pets 109

No Free Lunch 110

    Saying No 111

Birds 111

Rodents 112

Fish 113

Ferrets 114

Rabbits 115

Reptiles 115

Chapter 10

Barn-Animal Care 119

Livestock Care 120

Fees 120

Services 121
Horse Care 122
    Horse Vital Signs .122
    Bad Signs 122
    Horse Handling. 123
    Horse Wounds 124
    Feeding Horses 124
Sheep and Goats. 125
Cows 126
Pigs. 127
Llamas and Alpacas. .127
Other Types of Charges 128
A Word about Barn Cats 128

Chapter 11
Jungle Fever 131
Chinchillas 132
Sugar Gliders 133
Hedgehogs. 133
Potbellied Pigs 134
Monkeys 134
Wallabies. 136
Marketing Specialized Knowledge 136

Chapter 12
Expanding Your Business 139
Some Questions 140
Pet Specialist. 140
Expanding Revenue, Not Customers 140
    More Services 141
    Products. 142
Expanding On-Site 143
    Expansion Considerations. 143
Thinking Outside the Box 144
    Office Care. 144
    Night Watch or Off-Hour Feeding 144
Ecommerce 144
A Bona Fide Kennel 145

Doggie Day-Care Service 146
Memorial Services 147
Franchises 147
Classes 148
    Training with or without the Pet Owner. 148
Rehab. 148
Pet Taxi Service 149
Other Home-Related Services 149
Get It in Writing. 149
Extra Services. 150
    Plant Care 150
    Cleaning. 151
    Shopping 151
    Dealing With Home-Maintenance Appointments 151
And in the End. 152

Appendix
Pet Business Resources 153
Books about Animals 154
Books about Starting a Small Business. 154
Websites. 155
Places to Get Pet-Sitting Experience. 155
Business Websites 156
Website Building 156

Glossary 157

About the Author. 159

Index 161

Preface

The world is full of many kinds of people, ranging from those who can't wait to open their own business to those who would like to but are terrified by the thought. Of course, many people fall somewhere in between: those who definitely intend to start a business but are a bit nervous about it. Perhaps that describes your current situation.

The prospect of leaving a full-time job and its steady income can be a source of great anxiety for the would-be entrepreneur. Such a dramatic change can put anyone's nerves on edge! However, the following best practices for a business startup can alleviate a good amount of the startup jitters. In a world where even a quick jaunt to the grocery store can be fraught with complications, the hassle and risk associated with starting your own business might seem downright foolhardy.

But if you love animals and have always wanted to have a career working with them, this might be the perfect impetus for starting your own business. You've also dreamed of owning your own business. Running a pet business is fast becoming a viable way not only to earn a living but also to be your own boss and make a profit! It's a relatively simple business to manage, and if you love pets, especially cats, you might say it's purr-fect.

Note that pet businesses, especially pet-sitting, fall under the category of a service business, not unlike hair cutting, cosmetology, and auto detailing.

Pet-focused businesses also don't take a huge amount of money in startup costs. At its most basic, you can get going with some word-of-mouth advertising and reliable transportation. And if you live in a city, that transportation can be as cheap as bus or subway fare!

In a city, you'll find a wide variety of pets to take care of, from dogs and cats to lizards and ferrets. In part because of the multitude of cat photos on the internet, people have become friendlier to felines. As for city vs. country dogs, you might find fewer dogs in some cities, but city dogs need a lot more care than dogs living in the country. This includes daily walks both for exercise and for the animals to relieve themselves. Pets in rural areas—farm dogs and barn cats—usually don't need much in the way of pet-sitting. Often this is because real farm folks don't go anywhere—as the old saying goes, it takes a week to catch up from a day away from the farm! But the suburbs—ah, the suburbs—are a pet business owner's dream! People in the suburbs often left the heart of the city precisely so they could have pets and a yard. These communities are teeming with people who need someone to watch Fido while they commute to work elsewhere. Many of these clients also spoil their pets rotten, so there's a robust market for pet products and additional services like grooming and poop scooping.

The COVID-19 pandemic jolted the pet care industry in both directions. First it brought on a wave of new pet ownership, with many people getting a "pandemic pet." These new pet owners may need someone to watch their pets should they return to work outside the home. Odd schedules of employment and a "gig" economy, along with greater concern for pets left home alone, have prompted more people to pay someone to take on the job of watching their beloved pet.

On the flip side, the vast increase in the number of people working from home has also seen pet owners decide that now that they're home more often, they can take care of their pets throughout the day. Some pet sitters and pet-sitting services have, as a result, seen a sharp downturn in their businesses. Pet-care businesses such as Rover and PocketSuite were hit hard during the pandemic with Rover having to let go of 41 percent of their employees, while PocketSuite saw a 40 percent decline of bookings for dog walkers, and pet sitters, during the first two months of the pandemic. However, only a few months later, the business had returned to its prepandemic numbers. Why? Because those dog owners who no longer needed dog walkers or sitters spent the same money on having their pets groomed and/or trained.

What this means is that while those who return to the office, including many new pet owners, will need dog walking or pet sitting, it may be to your advantage to read about all the other offerings you can provide in the new world of homebased employees. This may be a great time to offer a wide array of pet-care products and add additional services to your offerings from grooming and training to taking animals to and from vet visits, to shopping for pet food and other items (which may include a few things the humans need) for your clientele. Rather than a few clients you see every day, you may need to have more clients whom you see once or twice a week—this will also be the case with clients who are returning to work only two days a week. If you love pets (which is part of the reason you're in this business), you need to focus on increasing your services and seek out more part-time or occasional customers to succeed in the new world of business.

This book lets you in on the ups and downs of the pet industry, especially pet caretaking and pet-sitting. It can be relatively easy to get started. But you also need to be realistic about the idiosyncrasies of the business. The job is demanding, both in time and responsibility. Besides being good with animals, you must also be an excellent time manager. Last but not least, you need to have all the skills that every business owner needs—such as customer-service skills, organizational skills, and the ability to keep good records. You must be prompt and reliable and diligent in collecting payments.

Being trustworthy is also a key to your success. Your clients are entrusting precious members of their families to you. They need to feel confident that you will show up when you say you will, that you will take good care of their pets, and that they can entrust you with the keys to their homes and all the contents in them. That's a big responsibility.

That said, a pet-focused business can be one of the most rewarding businesses to run. All the pet experts interviewed for this book brought up one critical point: by helping people take good care of their pets, you can feel good about your job. How many people can say that?

Other pet-related businesses are increasing in popularity and success on par with pet-sitting. Making pet-related products, such as all-natural dog biscuits, cat toys, and pet sweaters, can be a moneymaking venture. Pet massage, pet therapy, obedience training, day-care facilities, and almost anything else you can think of are potentially successful businesses. People are willing to pay to give a pet just about anything they are willing to give themselves.

We cover these opportunities, too, as a way to broaden your business and increase your profits. So if pet-sitting per se isn't your thing, chances are you still can find a rewarding business to start and run in the pet industry.

Your Customers Are Human

You love animals. You would love to work for yourself. *Why not*, you think, *combine the two in some sort of animal-related business?* Good idea.

You could start many kinds of animal-related businesses—a grooming salon, a doggie day-care facility, a pet supply shop. But these kinds of businesses can get expensive—they require real estate and inventory. (We'll talk about these more intense startup businesses in a later chapter.) In terms of startup costs, pet-sitting takes us back to one of the least expensive animal-related businesses you can start.

And then there's the issue of marketing. Let's say you begin to design brochures. But wait—suddenly you realize no pets on the planet will be reading your brochures. You need to appeal not to the pet, but to the pet's owner—who is, of course, human. It is with humans that you will be discussing the details of your service over the phone and online and from whom you will be getting payment.

stat fact

Current statistics vary widely, but approximately 89.7 million dogs and 95.6 million cats live in the U.S. today. According to the ASPCA, 68 percent of American households include at least one pet.

Pet-sitting is considered part of the service industry. The service industry isn't for everyone. Providing people with a service can be frustrating at best and hair-pulling at worst! People are picky (and if you aren't the people-pleasing type, customers can drive you downright crazy).

Of course, while the pet owner is away, you will be fulfilling your original intent—interacting with animals. In fact, Eva and Dorothy of DEPetWatch, in New York, found that after their initial interaction with the pet owner, which can be somewhat involved, the lion's share of their contact is with the pets, except for the scheduling of new appointments.

So a word to the wise: With a pet-sitting business, your marketing efforts are directed toward humans, not animals. If the fact you'll have to deal with people is OK with you, let's continue!

Where to Start?

The steps to starting a pet-sitting business are the same as any other business. You need to:

- ▶ Determine if a market for your business exists in your area.
- ▶ Determine what you want out of your business, both financially and professionally.
- ▶ Choose an organizational structure.
- ▶ Choose a name (and check to see if it is available).
- ▶ Create a concise business plan if you are looking for investors.
- ▶ Get financing, if necessary.
- ▶ Obtain the appropriate licenses and permits.
- ▶ Set up your base of operations.

- ▶ Create a website (and check if the web address is available).
- ▶ Create marketing materials to attract customers.

Every business needs a structure and a base of operations. Service businesses are often uncomplicated, and a startup can be less expensive than other kinds of businesses. You don't need the inventory that you would require to open a retail business or the equipment necessary for most offices. Occasionally, a service business needs some piece of specialized equipment—for instance, if you were to do rug cleaning. And with pet-sitting, you may find it's more convenient if you keep some pet supplies stocked in your car, but most everything you need for pet-sitting is supplied by the pet's owner. We'll get to the above points in detail in other chapters throughout this book. But before you spend time and money designing a fancy website and sending out brochures in your local area, you must ask yourself an important question: *Is there a market for a pet-sitting business in my area?*

Is Anybody Home?

You hope not! For pet-sitting, you are looking for pet owners who are away from home at least occasionally, if not regularly.

First, you need to determine where your demographic area begins and ends. Look at how many residential communities are within a few miles of your home. Keep in mind that the farther you have to drive, or commute to and from your customers (the pet owners), the less you are earning. Once you determine how far you can travel without cutting into your profits, you can focus on the various communities by studying their demographics.

Look more closely for neighborhoods with private homes in kid-friendly areas. Families often have a pet or two or three. You can also locate where the pets are by driving around areas in the mornings or after nine-to-five work hours to see if a lot of people are walking their dogs. Check out nearby parks to see if you can find a dog park. Pet-sitting customers do have a few common characteristics. The main one is that they are almost always gainfully employed. And there is no better customer to have in any business than one who earns a steady income! The second thing is that your customers are away from home either occasionally or often. How often people in a given area travel is hard to find in the demographics.

The two key reasons that people are away and are looking for a pet-sitter are work and vacation. Many pet-sitting customers need to travel for their jobs. They make enough money at that job and have paid vacation time, which means they want to go on vacation a couple of times a year in addition to a few long weekends. Most of those instances— business travel and vacation travel—are not appropriate for pets to come along.

Most pet-sitting customers consider their pets to be part of the family and want to ensure that their pets are well cared for. Many people feel their pets are more content if they stay in the comfort of their own home rather than go to a kennel while they travel. They recognize that pets do well in familiar surroundings and benefit from having someone around. That's where you come in!

Determine Your Demographics

How do you find out if gainfully employed pet owners exist in sufficient numbers in the area you would like to designate as your market? Along with online and in-person research, the following are some possibilities:

tip

Consider working for the competition before you start your own pet-sitting business. Be upfront about your intentions—if you are good enough, your competitor will be happy to have reliable backup when they are booked and can't take a job for a good client.

- ▶ Are there pet stores in the area(s)? If so, how busy are they? Besides finding online locations, you might go in and talk to the owners. You can ask if they have customers who have inquired about pet-sitting services. Perhaps there's a bulletin board where you can put a flier or your business cards once you have them made.
- ▶ How many veterinarians does the area support? In some areas, new veterinary hospitals are popping up every year. Again, look them up online, and stop by veterinary offices or animal hospitals some weekday afternoon (when they are least busy) and ask the staff at the front desk if they get questions from clients regarding reliable pet-sitters. Veterinary offices can be your biggest allies, either through word-of-mouth or simply by leaving a flier or business card on their bulletin board or, if they don't mind, a stack of business cards on their counter.
- ▶ Are there large businesses in your area? Are there large professional office parks with lots of white-collar businesses?
- ▶ Check with your local chamber of commerce. The staff's knowledge of businesses in the community can help.

Cat Fight or Mutual Grooming?

What if there is already a pet-sitting business established in the area you would like to serve? Do you toss your idea? Hardly.

Look at the number of competitive pet-sitting businesses in the area that you are looking to cover. The larger the area, the more likely there will be space for new pet-sitting businesses.

Call the competition as a pet owner (don't tell them you're going into the business) and simply ask some questions about their services for "Fido," your pretend 5-year-old dog. Ask about their rates and availability, and read any and all reviews you can find about each pet-sitting service in your area. Keep in mind that whatever they're doing wrong or are getting complaints about are things you will need to take note of to make sure you do them right. The competition's weaknesses become your strengths.

Pet-sitting is a unique business venture, even among other service businesses. You should make an effort to get to know some other pet-sitters. They can use you as a backup when they're not available, and you can use them as referrals for when you are too busy or simply unavailable on certain days. In pet-sitting, your schedule is dictated by your customers. If your customer calls and says they're headed for Atlanta on Friday for a four-day conference and need you to look after their pets, you can't tell them you're too busy, but you'll book them for the following weekend. If you are, in fact, too busy, you could refer them to someone else, who will hopefully return the favor. When you do these kinds of referrals, you do take the risk of losing a customer to the referral.

The Odd Dog Out

You want to think of ways to distinguish yourself from other pet-sitting businesses in the area. Perhaps there are already ways in which you are different—your credentials, your experience, your personal background. Be sure to promote these unique traits in your marketing materials. If your business goes beyond dogs and cats and includes farm animals, and you grew up on a thoroughbred racehorse farm in the middle of Kentucky bluegrass country, don't keep that fact hidden deep in your resume. Flaunt it on your flier and let potential customers know that you have particular expertise that the competition does not. If you are available at times in which much of your competitors are not, that also bodes well.

What Do Humans Want?

In any service-oriented business, there are key things that customers want. But when you are taking care of their pets, you need to provide these things in spades. What are they?

Reliability

When you agree to meet the client at 10:00 A.M., get there at 9:50. Always be on time, preferably even a little early. If it's an area with difficult parking, take a reconnaissance mission and find out if there's a municipal lot nearby or where easily accessible parking is available. Some cities have parking apps, while in other cities, such as New York, you may be best not driving, so look for mass transit to the neighborhood in which your client resides and give yourself enough time to take the subway or bus. Your clients may not worry if they arrive home from work at 6:00 P.M. or 7:30 P.M. to let their dog out, but they care what time you arrive if they are paying you to get there at 6:00 P.M. to care for their pet. Reliability is first and foremost in this business!

Trust

Pet owners need to feel you can be trusted implicitly. This is the most critical element of a pet-sitter's resume. Not only are you taking care of beloved pets, but often you are entrusted with the key to the customer's home and access to all its contents.

You can instill this trust in many ways—through your advertising, your marketing materials, your website, and your demeanor both in person and over the phone. Each point of contact with the public is an opportunity for you to build trust. You will certainly be expected to provide character references, and you should have a list of people ready who can vouch for you at a moment's notice. These can be former employers from other jobs, teachers, people whom you've worked with on charitable projects, etc. Be sure to forewarn those people that you are starting a pet-sitting business and that you are putting their names on your reference list. If a potential client calls, you don't want your reference to sound surprised and stammer to come up with some appropriate comments because they haven't seen you in years.

You can also offer to take care of some cats and dogs for free for friends and neighbors so they can say some nice (and honest) things about you when people call for references. If you've watched a neighbor's pet several times, perhaps they'll be perfect for a testimonial on your website.

Confidence

To woo customers for pet-sitting, you need to gain their confidence. They need to believe that not only are you trustworthy enough to be given a key to their home, but you are completely, utterly, and totally reliable. How do you do that? By being completely, utterly, and totally reliable. And then let those customers who have the utmost confidence in you spread the word! Once your business is up and running, you can begin to use your existing clients as references for potential customers and add to those testimonials.

Professionalism

As with any business, you need to be professional. That doesn't mean your business cards can't have a picture of a fluffy little Pomeranian with a bow in her hair on it—in this business, they can! But you want to have business cards, brochures, perhaps a few ads in appropriate free giveaway local newspapers, and a website that looks professional, yet also pet friendly—all of which make you seem like you are neat, reliable, and professional. We'll cover all your print and web needs in Chapter 4 when we do a deep dive on marketing.

Be sure to give estimates and invoices in print and on professional stationery. Don't be loosey-goosey with your communication—if you are, a client may feel you are also going to be sloppy with getting to their house to walk their dog at the appointed hour.

Also, you need to look professional when you meet clients and potential clients in person. But a professional-looking pet-sitter doesn't dress in a business suit! Khakis, clean jeans, T-shirts or knit polo shirts, and sturdy walking shoes or sneakers are probably more appropriate attire. You don't want to appear looking like you will be offended if Fifi jumps all over you and scratches your skirt, or if Bob, the long-haired Burmese cat, rubs half his coat on your raw silk pants. Look like you would be willing to get down on your knees and greet the dog or crawl under the porch to reach the cat in his hiding place when the neighbor's dog chases him under there. But try not to look like you just did all that. It's a fine line, but in general, business casual is appropriate attire in this business.

Customer Care

All businesses have the opportunity to make customers feel either dispensable or important. Choose the latter every time, and you will retain old customers and gain new ones easily.

► Always be Charged and Ready

In a business like this, you will use your cell phone often. You need to be reachable at a moment's notice. Get back to people quickly. Treat your cell phone like a piece of business equipment. You need the battery life and the value your phone offers to keep your business active and effective. If you waste the battery with personal activities like excessive texting or playing games while on the clock, it'll cost you more than the need for an extra charge. If your battery runs out, your business can suffer. Have a car charger or rechargeable fuel rod on hand, and/or be able to charge your phone at your clients' homes (ask them if it's OK first). Better yet, always charge your battery before going to work!

The simplest thing you can do is return people's calls promptly. It may sound obvious and simple, but it is also one of the most important things you can do to make customers feel appreciated. Another seemingly little thing you can do is remember your customers' pets' names (and your customers' names as well, of course!). Have their names readily available on your phone. You also want to be consistent in what you tell people. If you're available on Tuesday, be available on Tuesday—sure, an emergency can come up, but don't make appointments you cannot keep or be irresponsible when it comes to your clients. This takes us back to the need for reliability.

Giving Good Customer Service

All businesses deal with customers. Good customer service is the key to a successful business. How do you give good customer service in the pet-sitting business? It all starts with the phone, perhaps an email, and ends with excellent pet care. As you read through this book and get ideas for building and developing your business, always keep your customers in mind.

The steps are simple:

▶ *Make a good first impression.* Potential clients will probably contact you the first time by email. Get back to them quickly and set up a time to talk by phone. If they text, text back quickly—again, try to move the text to a conversation. This is the easiest way to ask and answer questions quickly. If you are not able to answer the phone, be sure to have a warm but businesslike personal voicemail greeting that tells them you will get back to them promptly, which should mean within 24 hours, if not within an hour or two. Let's face it—pets sleep at some point, giving you a chance to make a return call or text.

▶ *Be accessible.* You might think that prospective customers consider you a busy person with a successful business if they can never get in touch with you, but in the service industry, this will likely work against you. Pet-sitting may mean that you are on the road a lot, but don't expect customers to figure out what your daily schedule is like.

▶ *Respond to people quickly.* Check your calls, emails, and texts often. You might even be able to squeeze in a return call while today's client's Lhasa apso is wandering around the yard looking for the best place to do his business. Don't, however, talk long while you are working. Tanya K., a New Hampshire pet-sitter, chooses to shut her cell phone off when she is on a job to avoid being distracted. Just leave a message letting the prospective client know you have received their call and you will be in touch shortly. If the call is from a current client—not just someone you sit for occasionally, but someone for whom you are pet-sitting that very day—call back immediately. In many cases, a client will text something like "Are you around this weekend?" You just need to respond that you are or are not, depending on your schedule. Perhaps you can rearrange that schedule—if that's the case, let them know and work quickly before they call another pet-sitter.

▶ *Have answers to clients' and prospective clients' questions.* People have specific questions and concerns about hiring someone to take care of their pets. Have answers to these questions. Occasionally someone will stump you. But if someone asks if you know how to give shots to a diabetic cat, you should have an answer. Don't say "Well, I'm not sure." If you can do so, and have done this before, say so. If you have never given shots, you should also say so but add that you are willing to learn if the pet owner would like to teach you. (If the pet owner can do it, so can you.) Don't charge extra to make a visit to learn how to give the injection; consider it a useful tool that you can use with other clients. Read more about situations such as this in Chapter 5.

Pest Control

In a service business, you are especially prone to having a small percentage of customers who want to take up the largest percentage of your time. In fact, there is a well-known principle called the 80-20 Rule that states 80 percent of your business will come from 20 percent of your clients. If these "regular" customers pay well and don't take advantage of you (by frequently canceling at the last minute), they can make your business run a lot more smoothly. You can establish a pretty regular schedule. Remember, your customers are the key to the financial viability of your business. That makes them a necessary and valuable component, but it also means each customer has to *make* you money, not cost you money.

If, for instance, you are spending two hours each week on the phone with Mrs. Smith discussing the details of Fluffy's bowel movements the day you took care of him, or Mrs. Smith calls you back seven times to make sure you remember to go by her house Friday afternoon to take care of Fluffy, this is time consuming. Your time needs to be compensated. At first, you may let Mrs. Smith be a little neurotic about a new person taking care of Fluffy. But after you have proven yourself reliable and she has become confident in your services (exhibited by her willingness to use you repeatedly), you need to make sure that Mrs. Smith's business is in fact earning you money, not costing you.

Here are three simple ways to deal with difficult, time-sucking clients:

1. *Take control of the conversation when they call.* You need to be the one who determines when you hang up. This can become a bit of an art—you don't want to hang up on them because that may hurt your chances of repeat business. But you need to make it clear that you have things to do and leave the conversation on a pleasant note. The same holds true with endless texts—you don't want to be rude, but you need to make it clear that you are busy and cannot continue to read texts at this time.

2. *Increase the fee you charge the client.* You can tell them your general rates have gone up, or you can explicitly charge for follow-up phone time exceeding one 15-minute call or endless text messages.

3. *Finally, you can be blunt with a time-consuming customer.* If you are a master of diplomacy—and you should be if you are going to start any service business—simply find a polite but firm way to tell them that they take up too much of your time with repeated calls and that you are happy to chat with them once after your visit, or text briefly, but more than that requires an additional charge.

You can also offset the phone calls or texts in a couple of ways. You should plan to leave a follow-up note with every client to let them know what you did throughout the day and if anything occurred that might seem unusual. Pet-sitter Amy C. in Maine is adamant about the importance of leaving notes for owners after each pet-care visit. Perhaps with Mrs. Smith, you should take a couple of minutes to leave notes that are longer than usual and see if that is enough to offset a phone call from her. You might also try making a follow-up call to her before she calls or texts you. This gives you control of the call and you are calling her on your schedule—which may not be perfect for her, so she may be quite willing to make the call a quick one if you caught her just before she was leaving the house for an appointment. In fact, figuring out when she may be busy—perhaps, you learn she plays bridge every Thursday evening at 7:00—and calling her a half hour before she usually leaves the house can be a useful way to keep a call short.

tip

If your area has a lot of hotels, determine which ones allow pets. Post your fliers or leave business cards there. Guests with pets may retain your services to tend to their pet while they go sightseeing for the afternoon. You need to have access to professional services, such as veterinary care, to enable people to feel comfortable entrusting their pet to a stranger in a strange town, but it just might be a perfect niche!

Sometimes, unfortunately, it may just pay to drop a customer from your books. If the person is too much of a pain in the neck, there is also the likelihood that same person will become annoyed with you over something and give you bad local reviews, spread negative word-of-mouth, or even increase the potential for a lawsuit. Some people cannot be satisfied and just aren't worth the effort.

Are You Ready?

Are you trustworthy, professional, and reliable? Do you instill confidence about your abilities as a pet caretaker and your interest in animals? Then keep reading, you've got a business to run!

Putting the Parts of Your Business in Place

How you set up your pet-sitting business is critical to your success. Only you know how you like to work. If you are going to work for yourself, you might as well set things up to suit you!

Many people who go into business working for themselves work from home and then set up their days just as if they were working in an office for someone else. If that is how you need to arrange your business to accommodate your customers, then that's what you should do. But pet-sitting doesn't need to conform to a nine-to-five schedule, nor should it. Pet-sitting can be day and/or night.

You may not have any pressing business during the middle of the day, but this is no reason to sit on your hands. In later chapters, we explore marketing materials and advertising that you could be creating, or financial information that you could be recording or analyzing, but right now, let's see how your business might be constructed.

The Name Game

Your business needs a name—one that people can remember. Start looking at other pet-sitting business names in your area. You do this for two reasons. First, you don't want a name someone already has—they have probably registered as a business using that name and have a similarly titled website. Second, you may get some ideas. Because pets are cute, many pet-sitting services go with something short and cute. The website https://toughnickel.com lists 50 pet-sitter business names, including: Waggity Tails Pet Sitting, Fuzzy Faces Pet Sitters, Woof Meow Pet Sitting, Muddy Paws Pet Service, Claws N' Paws Pet Sitting, Woof N' Wag Pet Sitting, and K9 to 5 Pet Sitters. You'll also find names like Little Rascals Doggie Day Care, Pet Sit Pros, and Paw-Sibly the Best. Of course, you might decide to provide some information in the name, such as Arlington Dog and Cat Sitters or Francine's Exotic Pet-Sitting Service. If you do more than sitting, mention it—for example, Paula's Pet-Sitting and Grooming.

As you'll notice, most pet-sitting service names are about four words. Leave words like "best" or "cheapest" out of your name because you can't prove it. Write a bunch of ideas down, and then ask your friends, family, or anyone who'll listen what names they like best. You might want to check out *The Naming Book* by Brad Flowers (Entrepreneur Press, 2020).

Once you narrow down some name ideas, test-market the name with pet owners. Take your time—you want a name that people will remember.

Business Setup

First, you need to address the nasty little topic of business structure. Several possibilities exist.

▶ *Sole proprietorship.* This is the route that most pet-sitting businesses take, especially if you are working part time and/or homebased. The good news about this setup

▶ Four Tips for Getting Into the Pet-Sitting Groove

1. Set aside a work area devoted to your business, even if it is just a small computer desk in the corner of your living room with a wall schedule and shelving to hold supplies. You will feel more organized when talking with potential clients and doing your bookkeeping. Your family will also be happy that your business is not spread all over the house.

2. Don't procrastinate about tasks you need to keep up with, such as bookkeeping. Either do a little every day so you don't get overwhelmed, or bite the bullet and hire someone to do it for you. You could pay someone you know who is good with numbers to come by a couple of hours a week and keep your records up-to-date. However, with the glut of bookkeeping software programs, you could set one up in an hour and only need a little time here and there to fill in the numbers.

3. Figure out your business hours and put your business first during those hours. For a pet-sitter, you will probably find that your busiest hours are first thing in the morning, midday, and late afternoon/early evening—taking care of people's pets at the beginning and end of the day, and the lunchtime walks for nine-to-five pet owners. Don't schedule appointments and activities during those times; leave them free for your business. You don't want to spend your time making doctor, dentist, and hairdresser appointments and rescheduling them because you got a job during that time. If the day arrives and you don't have a client lined up, use the time to prospect for new clients, do some research, or read that week's barrage of pet- and business-related blogs and web posts.

4. Keep looking for potential clients even when you have a pretty full calendar. It's hard to predict how many clients you will have throughout a given year. You may have 50 clients on your mailing list, people for whom you have actually done pet-sitting. But of those 50 clients, perhaps only 30 will use your services in the course of one year. This is a business with a fair amount of turnover. Some clients will move. Others will have a family member take over your job because their schedule now allows for them to spend more time with their pet(s). You may be replaced by a kind neighbor who recently retired and has time on their hands. And, sadly, some pets will die. You're better off with a waiting list for your services or expanding by adding a second pet-sitter to your business than you are by simply turning down new clients.

is that it is simple. The business is just you—you make the decisions, and you get all the revenue. You also put up all the money, and you risk all your own personal assets. That's the bad news of sole proprietorship.

▶ *Partnership*. A partnership structure means that you and one or more other people are the owners/managers of the business. Dorothy and Eva, pet-sitters from New York, have a partnership business. Both consider the business a full-time career, and each has a full complement of customers. Note: even if you're related or best friends, sign an agreement that spells out what you each do, and how you can amicably get out of the partnership if necessary.

▶ *Limited partnership*. This is where you are the main owner/manager and your partner (or partners) is a silent investor. The benefit of any type of partnership is that you have someone to share everything with—the liability, the decision making, and the work. The downside of the partnership structure is that you have someone to share everything with—e.g., the revenue. So it can be harder to make money, but the theory is that two heads are better than one. The tax structure is also better with a partnership—no small consideration.

▶ *Corporation*. The most appealing part about incorporating is that the corporation becomes the entity that is at risk, not you personally. It can be a little expensive to set up a corporation, mostly because you will typically need to hire a lawyer. The downside of a corporation is that it typically involves a lot of paperwork, plus you may have corporate taxes to pay on top of your personal income taxes. Ask a lawyer before incorporating, and they will help you determine whether it is worthwhile and, if so, which type of corporation would best meet your needs.

How you structure your business will depend on whether you are on your own or with partners, and what your future goals are. You might ask your accountant and/or your attorney for their opinions.

McPet Sitter?

The other possibility to consider for your business structure is buying into a pet-sitting franchise. Opportunities in pet-related franchises are multiplying as people become increasingly willing to spend money on frills for their dogs and cats. One of the closest analogies in service business franchising is Merry Maids housecleaning service. This business has one main thing in common with pet-sitting: People are entrusting you to come into their homes.

Certainly, a key benefit of buying into a franchise is that you get immediate name recognition. But other benefits exist as well, depending on the franchise. These could include training, marketing materials, a procedures manual, support from an experienced team, and startup loans to make it easier to open your business. They offer a turnkey starting point so you can step into the role without having to start from square one. They also provide customers with a sense of security by having a brand name.

Some disadvantages of a franchise may come in terms of control—the franchise has it; you don't. Typically, a franchise determines where your business is located, although with pet-sitting, this isn't as much of an issue. They may have a say in what territories you cover though.

Franchises handle nearly all marketing elements—from the advertising you can use to signage to what products you offer for sale. The parent company has a firm say in what your target market can be because the company wants to sell as many franchises as possible and doesn't want you to squeeze into another potential market. If control is important to you, then you might be better off starting an independent business.

Franchises can be expensive to buy into, so you really need to decide if it is worth the investment. Here are some expenses you can expect to pay:

▶ An initial investment fee, usually several thousand dollars
▶ An ongoing "royalty" fee, where you pay a percentage of your sales to the parent franchise
▶ An advertising fee or co-op advertising dollars—you pay your share of the franchisor's overall national advertising campaigns

You should definitely investigate the franchise as carefully as possible with the Better Business Bureau for any complaints registered against the franchise, and check if it has ever filed for bankruptcy or had other court-related proceedings. You should check online reviews of the franchise and retain a lawyer to read over the fine print of the contract. You want to know upfront what every possible cost will be.

If you are more the type who likes to do the work and not the type who likes to create things, then a franchise situation may work great for you.

Popular pet-sitting franchises in the U.S. include:

▶ Pet Sit Pros: Based in California
▶ Out-U-Go!: Based in Chicago
▶ Snaggle Foot: Based in the Midwest and East
▶ Fetch! Pet Care: Nationwide
▶ Sitter4Paws: Located in Florida, southern California, and Arizona

▶ In Home Pet Services: Based in New York

▶ Camp Bow Wow: Nationwide (includes doggie day care)

Pet-Sitting in Clients' Homes

Taking care of your clients' pets in their homes is probably the way that most of your clients will be cared for. Studies have shown, and logic prevails, that pets are more comfortable remaining in their own homes when their humans are away rather than being shuttled off to a kennel.

tip

Check your phone often for texts, emails, or calls. You never know when a client might be desperate for a last-minute service. You don't want to miss a job just because you didn't check your messages. And if the client tries another pet-sitting service to fill that emergency need, you might have just lost a client!

Pet care in the pet's home environment creates many variables you need to be aware of. First, it requires a visit when the owner is still at home to become familiar with the pet's home setup. Get the grand tour. Find out where the food is, where the owner allows the pet to roam in the house, where the pet toys are stashed, and even the basics like how to get in and how to shut off the alarm system if there is one. Tanya K. in New Hampshire finds that the average initial consultation takes around an hour.

Doing home care while owners are away typically means you have to visit twice a day. This has a great bearing on how wide a range you accept as a market. If you have to drive twice a day to someone's house, make sure it isn't a 90-minute trip each way!

Making the Pet Environment Comfortable

You unlock the front door of the home where your weekend pet-sitting job is located. The thermostat has been set lower than it might be if the owners were home, but nonetheless, it seems significantly colder than you expected it to be. What do you do?

If it's January in Vermont, your customers will probably be grateful if you call the furnace company; a house that is left for a couple of days without heat in a Vermont winter will probably have frozen, and perhaps burst, pipes when the homeowners return from their weekend away.

If it's September in Vermont, frozen pipes will unlikely be an issue. Even if it drops slightly below freezing for one night, the interior of the house will probably remain above freezing. However, even though the pipes may not freeze, the pets in the home may be in jeopardy. Birds, some reptiles, and smaller animals are not able to deal with cold

▶ Smile!

Your cell phone camera can play a major role in your business. You can use this in some great ways to enhance your business: one is to take photos of you and your clients' pets to show how well you're getting along. Pet owners love photos of their pets! Text them some photos of you and their pet playing or of something funny. If they're worried, you can reassure them during their travels that all is well at home. But don't overdo it; there's a line between cute and annoying.

Second, you'll have some photos saved to post if the pet, heaven forbid, ran off, so other people can see what the pet looks like. You can also use photos on your website (owner permitting) to show potential clients some of the pets you sit for and how well you get along.

temperatures. Getting that furnace running again may mean the difference between life and death for the pet who has been entrusted to your care. And if the furnace is not running properly, the malfunction could cause carbon monoxide buildup or danger of fire, so it is best to call in a professional.

How that pet fares under your care will certainly have an impact on your continued relationship with that client and may have an impact on your business overall. Remember, satisfied customers tell a couple of people on average; unsatisfied customers tend to tell a couple of dozen people!

Pet Care in Your Own Home

We cover creating a separate kennel at your home in Chapter 12, "Expanding Your Business." In lieu of opening a kennel, let's talk about the benefits of performing pet care right in your own home. The overhead would be nominal, you wouldn't have to do all that driving, and the pets would be happy because you would have more time for them, right? Well, maybe.

Like people, house pets get accustomed to their own home and their own routine. With their owner gone, their routine gets thrown out the window. Add to that a strange house, especially if you have pets of your own, and life can become a totally different deal.

The idea of pet-sitting with your clients' pets in your home should be thought over very carefully. It's one thing to take care of your mother's little dog while she is in Florida for two weeks. It's quite another to incorporate a strange pet into your household.

"Most people doing this are pet lovers and have too many pets of their own to take other people's animals into their homes," says Amy C. of Amy's Animal Care in Maine, adding that she rarely takes dogs into her house. "My dogs are just too active." If you are going to take pets into your home, do a test-run first. Have the other pet and their owner come to your house for a short "meet and greet." If the animals seem to get along well, you will probably be fine; if not, you'll need to pet-sit at the client's house. Dogs adjust to other dogs much more easily than cats to other cats. Some cats and dogs also react well together; others do not.

Pet-Sitting as a Side Job

If pet-sitting is a side job for you, a way to make extra money beyond your nine-to-five job, you may be able to expand your market to include areas near your job site. So perhaps you work an hour away from your home; in that case, it would make sense to take on jobs that are along your commute or near your office. Expanding your market to encompass your work area can make up some of the income you lose from the fewer clients you can take on. However, you'll want to keep a couple of items in mind with this sideline approach.

Are you in a job where you might get called away on a business trip at the last minute? If so, you cannot risk being called away the same week your client is out of town. You might be able to make up for this by having an assistant you trust who can fill in for you in a pinch or take up the slack if you get more clients than you can handle with a full-time job (although if that's the case, perhaps it's time to go into pet-sitting full time!). But remember, in a service business, your clients are hiring you personally as much as they are hiring a service. As the owner, you are responsible for all business activities.

If you were to arrive at your client's house to take care of the pets before heading to work, what would happen if there were something that required you to take extra time—perhaps the pet was injured overnight or seemed sick and in need of veterinary care or at least an hour or

tip

If you have an employee, you need an EIN—Employer Identification Number—issued by the Internal Revenue Service. You can apply online at www.irs.gov. Or you can send in Form SS-4. It is simple, fairly quick, and absolutely necessary for anything but the simplest sole proprietorship.

so of observation? Is your employer and/or your type of work flexible enough for you to be able to come in a couple of hours late without notice? What if this happened three times in one week? Would you be at risk of losing your regular job because of the part-time pet-sitting work? When you take responsibility for other people's pets, they need to take priority.

Can you stand adding two extra hours, maybe more, to your workday? Unless your pet-sitting service extends only to your neighborhood and you can walk across the yard in your slippers and pajamas to do your work, you need to be ready for work and on the road earlier than usual. And you need to stop and take time to tend to the pets under your care at the end of your long workday. If you are always just busting to get home, slip off your shoes, and relax with a glass of wine in front of the TV, adding an hour to the end of your workday may not be the right thing for you.

However, research shows that pets have the ability to cheer us up, make us smile, get words out of people who haven't talked for years, and allow elderly folks to remain active without caretakers. The positive benefits of interacting with animals are well-documented, so maybe tossing a ball for a client's dog for a half hour after work is just what you need to get to your own home in a better mood!

The bottom line is if you can fit pet-sitting into your routine, go for it, but don't try to take on something that you cannot commit to for the sake of some extra money. And if you do take on the job, make sure you're adhering to rules and regulations.

Don't Zone Out

Don't ignore local zoning ordinances about what you can or can't do when it comes to operating a business out of your home. And don't assume just because the guy up the street operates an accounting business from his home that it's legal to do so or that the same rules apply to a pet-sitting business. The accountant may be operating legally, but your home may come under different zoning laws, even if it's just a few yards or blocks away from the homebased accountant.

Typically, if your business doesn't need to have a sign posted at the end of your driveway or doesn't require clients coming to your home, you are probably going to be fine. Homebased businesses have grown by leaps and bounds. Millions of people work at home and nobody knows or cares. In your case, the work entails phone calls, posting on your website, emails, texts, bookkeeping, etc.

The real problem could occur if you are using your own home to pet-sit a wide range of animals. Then you may need to check the zoning ordinances. Complying with the zoning ordinances for your town or your part of town may be as simple as filing for a permit at a modest fee. Go to the town hall and ask questions about zoning ordinances or any other local laws or restrictions that may pertain to your business. Don't ask questions only of the town clerk. Talk to the chair of the zoning board, perhaps the planning board chair, and someone on the zoning board of adjustments. It can't hurt to cover all your bases. It is not worth spending money setting up your business only to find out that you can't operate from your home.

Do You Need a Business Plan?

It all depends on how you plan to proceed. If you are looking to build your own business as a solo enterprise, you may just need to maintain a comprehensive to-do list and some accurate record keeping to make sure you do what is necessary on a regular basis.

If you are looking to build a larger business with other employees and perhaps office space, or a kennel for dogs, you may need backers or investors, which means that you need a business plan. A business plan can help ensure a well-organized business with few, if any, surprises. It can help you get startup or expansion capital by showing the viability of your idea or the ways your business is set up to meet specific goals, as mapped out in your business plan, for the future.

A major function of your business plan is as a roadmap for you to keep on track with your planned destination, at both the macro and micro levels. If you refer to your plan often, it helps you see immediately where you got off track and allows you to get back on track before you get too far astray.

Many sources are available for getting help with your business plan (see the Appendix). Here we'll cover the basic elements you need in your plan.

Business Plan Information

Information about writing a business plan abounds. A number of websites and books are available that include samples of business plans (see the Appendix). Don't expect to simply use an existing pet-sitter's business plan and plug in your name in all the appropriate places. Find one with a format that appeals to you, and use the format as a template for writing your own business plan.

Much of the general business-related topics are the same in all business plans. You need to fill in the details as they relate specifically to pet-sitting. In fact, be sure your business plan reminds readers at all times what kind of business you are starting.

Keep your business plan short. Business plans are rarely 50 pages anymore, unless you're starting a major national company, which is unlikely. For your purposes, write a concise plan, especially if you want investors to actually read it. You can also use a business pitch to get investors interested. This is a popular way of presenting an overview of your business to an audience. Typically, this is done as a 15–25-minute PowerPoint presentation. Be ready to answer any possible question they could throw at you.

Executive Summary

This is where you succinctly spell out just what business you are starting. This is not where you go into details or spend time trying to convince the reader that your business is a good idea. Simply offer a well-thought-out and focused overview of what your business is. Often this section is written last, after you've completed the rest of the business plan.

Industry Overview

Provide information here on pet-sitting and pet industries. Statistics on the number of dogs/cats per household, how often pet owners tend to solicit pet-care services, and how the spending on pet care has increased dramatically over the past decade is convincing information that your business idea is a viable one.

Your Credentials

Include not only your animal-related credentials here, but also your experience in small business and business in general. Early in your business plan, you should include your resume or a bio. Elaborate on some of the jobs you've had and the skills you've acquired that help you in either running a small business or caring for pets. Those skills can be marketing successes (especially measurable ones), projects you helped launch that went on to be successful, or even examples of projects that required exceptional time management.

Operating Overview

This section covers exactly how you plan to set up your business, such as whether you will have an office in your home, whether you plan to rent a storage space, whether you plan to hire any help, what services you will provide, how much you will charge, and the territories in which you will serve clients.

Financials

All good business plans have financial projections of at least three—and preferably five—years out. Your forecasting can certainly be modest, but you want to show annual improvement or, at the very least, that you can hold your own over the first three years. Your financials include spreadsheets on revenue and expense projections and a balance sheet showing the difference between the two. If you are looking to grow or scale a business and are seeking outside investors, you would add a market analysis, competitive analysis, and possibly other financial documents.

As you can see, most of these elements are to generate interest from potential investors. Because the startup money required for this type of business is very low, you probably do not need a business plan until your business grows and/or you want to scale it to the next level (i.e., adding employees, office space, an inventory of pet friendly items, etc.). Instead, make comprehensive lists of what you need to do, as mentioned earlier, and if you need some money, look to family and friends, and simply present your well-thought-out ideas.

tip

If you are thinking of hiring someone to help out, check your local community colleges for a veterinary technician program. These are good places to post notices, and you will increase your chances of finding a dedicated and knowledgeable pet person!

Startup Costs

Startup costs for a pet-sitting business should be modest. The one major outlay you may have to consider is reliable transportation. If you are driving an older vehicle, you may need to consider upgrading—look at used cars or see if you can get a good deal on a lease from a local dealer. If you already have a reliable vehicle, make sure to do the maintenance to keep it in good running condition. You don't want to be stuck on the side of the road because your car broke down, leaving Rufus at home in dire need of a walk.

Your other key expense is marketing and promoting your business. This means making sure your laptop, tablet, desktop, or any other computer is fully functioning as necessary. Today, most business data is stored on computers and backed up onto external hard drives, in the cloud, or even on thumb drives—remember, it's very important (and inexpensive) to back up your data constantly. While it's fine to store data on your cell phone, it's still important to back it up. Phones can get lost, break, or get stolen. They can also run out of storage space.

You should be able to start a pet-sitting business for $5,000 or less, unless you need to buy new transportation. Figure 2–1 on page 25 outlines potential startup costs.

Forms

You've now learned that as a pet-sitter you need to be trustworthy, reliable, well-groomed, and incredible at time management. Don't stop trying to reach perfection yet—to be successful in this business, you also need to be organized.

One way to keep yourself organized is to use a few common forms. The Startup Expenses Worksheet on page 25 is a good example. You will surely come up with more of

Startup Expenses Worksheet

Pre-Startup	Cost
Legal services	$300
Startup (local) advertising	$200
Website design and hosting	$1,500
Equipment	
First-aid kit	$80
Pet items, including dog leashes and collars, pooper-scooper, pet toys, kitty litter, etc.	$170
Office Furnishings and Equipment	
Computer/printer	$1,500
Desk/chair	$200
Forms/business cards/invoices/paper/etc.	$200
Business insurance	$500
Miscellaneous	$350
Total Startup Expenses	**$5,000**

Of course, this is only the case if you are one of the rare few people who do not own a computer and *need* an office chair. Should you have a computer and a chair that meets your needs, you can get started for less.

FIGURE 2–1: **Startup Expenses Worksheet**

your own as you go along, but a few basic forms are important. Be careful not to create so many forms that you need a form to keep track of the forms.

Client and Pet Profiles

These are your documents that hold information about the clients and their pets. The client profile includes basic information, such as name, address, and home and work phone numbers. Figure 2–2 on page 27 is an eample of a client profile worksheet. Figure 2–3 on page 29 shows a pet profile worksheet. You can also use a customer relationship management (CRM) system or project management software to record this information.

You should include a section for each pet. The pet's info needs to be a little more detailed because the pet is who you are actually caring for. You want to know the pet's name, the feeding schedule, amount and type of food, and any feeding idiosyncrasies, such as needing to mix water in the dry food.

You definitely want to have a section where you can note any regular medication the pet needs. You need to include in your file:

▶ The name(s) of the medication
▶ How much the pet takes (dosage) and how often
▶ How it is typically administered
▶ Where the medicine is bought, especially if it is a prescription drug

If the pet has a chronic illness of any kind, and is currently sick or suffering from something that may crop up while under your care, you need to include this information. You'll want to know how old the pet is and how they typically behave. For instance, does the pet generally lie around the house all day, or are they usually energetic and eager to see people, even strangers? You might also make a few notes of how the pet behaved the day you came for the initial consultation.

Include on this basic information sheet any specifics about the household—is there a security system, and are there any tricks to using it? What day is garbage pickup? What furniture is the pet allowed on, if any? If you agree to do any basic home care, such as watering the plants or bringing in the mail, make note of those tasks, too.

Emergency Care

This should be on the same form and be succinct and clear—it shouldn't be so complicated and full of information that you can't readily find the key emergency information you need when an actual emergency arises.

Include the pet's veterinarian's number, the number for the animal control officer in town, the number of the animal hospital that the client uses or would use, and, of course, the cell phone number of the pet owner. Chances are the pet owner will leave all this information for you on the refrigerator or the counter, but you also want it in a place that you know you can readily find it. See Figure 2–4 on page 31 for an example of a form.

Store all your pet information files on your phone, back them up on your computer for safekeeping, and even have printed-out hard copies for all your pet clients.

Client Profile Worksheet

Date of initial contact: _____

Name: _____

Address: _____

City/state/ZIP: _____

Directions: _____

_____

Contact Information

Home phone: _____

Work phone 1: _____

Work phone 2: _____

Email address: _____

Cell numbers: _____

Additional contact info: _____

_____

Contact info for current trip: _____

_____

Most Common Reason for Service

____ Business travel

____ Vacation

____ Weekday lunch visit

____ "Emergency" visits (client unexpectedly calls)

____ Other

FIGURE 2–2: **Client Profile Worksheet**

Client Profile Worksheet

Pets _____

Type _____

Size _____

Age _____

   Pet 1: _____

   Pet 2: _____

   Pet 3: _____

   Pet 4: _____

(see other side for additional pets)

Do any pets have special medical needs? _____

_____

_____

_____

Do any pets require special handling? _____

_____

_____

_____

FIGURE 2–2: **Client Profile Worksheet,** continued

Pet Profile Worksheet

Update this sheet with every job; do one profile for every pet the client has, and if you are using your computer for the files, remember to back them up.

Pet name: _____

Owner name/address: _____

Type of animal: _____

Age: _____

Feeding

What brand and type of food does the pet eat? _____

Where is the pet's food typically purchased? _____

Feeding Instructions

____ Dry food and canned food mixed together.

____ Dry food and canned food fed in separate dishes.

____ Water in dry food.

____ Pet tends to eat food immediately and completely.

____ Pet tends to eat food over course of time.

____ Pet is a fussy eater.

Does the pet get treats regularly? _____

Does the pet have any dietary constraints? _____

(e.g., trying to lose weight, uses prescription-only foods, must have supplements)

Medications

Does the pet receive any medication? _____

What is the medication?_____

_____

FIGURE 2–3: **Pet Profile Worksheet**

Pet Profile Worksheet

What is it for? _____

Where is the medication kept? _____

How frequently is it administered? _____

How is it administered? _____

What is the source of the medication? _____

(veterinarian or regular drugstore)

Behavior

Does the pet have any behavioral idiosyncrasies? _____

_____

Does the pet get along with all other pets in the household? _____

_____

Should the pet be separated from another pet when left alone? _____

_____

Is the pet well-socialized with other pets of its species? _____

_____

Exercise

What kind of regular exercise should the pet receive during the pet-sitting period?

_____

Attach Photo Here

(update photo annually, more often if pet is juvenile)

FIGURE 2–3: **Pet Profile Worksheet,** continued

Emergency Notification Regarding My Pets

In Case of an Accident or Death

In the event that I am incapacitated and unable to make my wishes known regarding my pets while I am away and they are under someone else's care, please honor the following requests: The welfare of my pets is a primary consideration.

DO NOT turn over to Animal Control.

Contact the following as soon as possible:

Cell number: _____   Work number: _____

If they cannot be reached, please contact:

Cell number: _____   Work number: _____

All expenses for the pets will be guaranteed by them.

If the pets are not injured, they are to be cared for by the nearest reputable boarding kennel and be kept in the best possible manner until arrangements can be made to get them home.

If the pets are injured, they are to be cared for by the nearest reputable veterinarian. I prefer that my veterinarian be contacted regarding decisions on the pets' care and treatment. My veterinarian has all my pets' medical records available and knows my wishes.

Contact my veterinarian:

Office number: _____   Night number: _____

Contact my pet-sitter: _____

Cell number: _____   Additional number: _____

My pet-sitter has the information and authority to care for my pets and knows whom to turn them over to. My pets can be released to my pet-sitter from any authorities.   _____ Initial

If any pet is injured beyond all hope of recovery, that pet is to be humanely euthanized.   _____ Initial

FIGURE 2–4: **Emergency Notification Regarding My Pets**

Emergency Notification Regarding My Pets

Photographs and descriptions of the pets are attached. For identification purposes, these pets are tagged or tattooed with an identifying number or have had a microchip ID implanted. _____

_____

Owner signature: _____ Date: _____

Name: _____

Address: _____

Home phone: _____ Work phone: _____

Cell phone: _____

Spouse/significant other: _____

Parents: _____

My pet's guardian: _____ Phone: _____

Courtesy Amy Carlson, Amy's Animal Care

FIGURE 2–4: **Emergency Notification Regarding My Pets,** continued

You may also want to put the pet's groomer in your file—although a skunk spraying is the only thing that comes to mind that could constitute a grooming emergency!

Startup and Operating Capital

You will need two kinds of money for your business venture:

1. *Startup money.* This is the amount of money you will need to begin to operate your business. The good news about pet-sitting, and many service businesses, is that the capital needed to get up and running is usually quite low—in fact, it can easily be

less than $5,000. You need only enough to get your website up and running, create some marketing materials, set up a separate phone line, buy the necessary supplies, take a couple of classes, and get your car completely serviced.

2. *Operating capital.* This is the money required to keep your business running until it begins to generate revenue. The goal is for the business to create its own operating capital. Your startup capital should be enough to last until your business generates revenue. But then you will need to have operating capital to keep supplies stocked, gas in the car, and furnish any other needs depending on what services you choose to offer.

Cash flow is very important in a business, especially one that runs on relatively small amounts of cash. Therefore, you need to make sure to have easily accessible cash available.

▶ Best Practices for Small Businesses

When running a small business, several "best practices" help your business lean in the direction of success. Here are six:

1. *Give money the respect it deserves.* You do not have to be embarrassed about making money, and you should not be shy about collecting it. Unless you are set up as a nonprofit (no easy task), no customer should expect a business to be unprofitable. Set your fees at a rate the market will bear and that will bring you the cash flow you need to create and maintain a good business. Giving service away or spending a half hour of time consulting on the phone for free can eat away at your profits. Time is money in business.

2. *Be proactive, and make sure you're compensated fairly for what you do.* Don't take personal checks from people (which could bounce), unless you know them well and have worked for them before. If you are not set up to take credit cards, let clients know in advance how they can pay you, which may include PayPal or Venmo, or that you simply take cash when your clients return home.

3. *Borrow as little as possible but as much as you need.* Undercapitalization is one reason small businesses fail. Another problem is giving away too many pieces of the pie. It's very easy to offer people a 10 percent stake in your business, or more, when you have nothing—but once you have money coming in, you'll regret that you gave so much of your profit away to backers. You need to keep your business running to get customers to bring in revenue and make your business a financial success. However, because startup costs are low for this type of business, why not set aside money before getting into the

▶ Best Practices for Small Businesses, continued

business and finance yourself as much as possible? Then borrow from friends and family so you can keep the interest rate very low. But don't take advantage of their generosity—pay them back as soon as you can.

4. *Maintain health insurance.* If your spouse has a job that provides benefits to you, awesome. But don't be without at least catastrophic insurance that would cover large hospital and emergency bills. If at all possible—although it's not easy for small-business owners—also maintain a disability policy that provides some level of coverage if you are injured and cannot perform the type of work that you do. This is typically quite expensive and isn't necessary if your income is not essential to your family's well-being. But if it is, do some research and find a policy. (See Chapter 6 for more information on this.)

5. *Be realistic about how much business you can take on.* Burnout is one of the top factors in why small businesses close down—the owner/manager simply wears out! This often happens within the first 18 months. While this is not to say that any small-business owner can afford to be accused of being lazy, committing 18 hours a day, six or seven days a week is exhausting, plain and simple. If your plan is to start your business, make it phenomenally successful, and sell it within two years, perhaps this will work. But if you are planning to be in it for the long haul, building up gradually and perhaps selling or retiring in ten or 15 years, start slowly with a few customers and increase your business as you gain experience.

6. *Hire employees sparingly.* Employee's paychecks as well as contributions for Social Security, workers' compensation, and unemployment taxes add up fast. When you think you need an employee to walk or house-sit some of your client's pets, or to help you with paperwork or bookkeeping, do a thorough financial breakdown, preferably with your accountant, and make sure the employee will pay for themself through either increased or more efficient business in a relatively short time, say, within six months. Do thorough interviews and get references from any potential employee so it doesn't become a nightmare. In this type of business, you will likely find some part-timers whom you can try out to see if they are responsible and good employees—remember, when you hire people to work for you, it is your reputation that is on the line. Don't let someone else tear down the good reputation you have built. As they say, hire slowly (and carefully) and fire quickly.

Obtaining Financing

Although a startup pet-sitting business requires only modest startup funds compared with many other businesses, if you need to approach a lender for a loan, it can go a long way if you have your financial projections or statements in order and present them professionally as part of your loan request. Applying for a loan can be stressful enough, so being ahead of the game with a full complement of financial statements from your business plan will save you some headaches. You also want a figure in mind; this is how much you actually need to get started. This should be broken down to cover each expense your business needs as a startup. Don't try to slip in some extra funds so you can take a short vacation or for any other perks. Loan officers are not looking to give you a loan in the first place, so make sure they see that you need it, have some kind of collateral to pay it off, and are not in debt.

warning

While growth is the desired goal in any business, be sure your business growth is not too fast—too many customers, too many expenses, too many employees. Businesses measure growth in different ways. Growth can mean higher revenue, more clients, more employees, expanding your reach, or all of the above.

Basic Services

A ny service business needs to offer certain basic, expected services. Pet-sitters also need to have a core offering that your customers can expect.

The four basic services you provide for pet owners are:

1. Feeding.

2. Making sure a dog gets out to do his business or a cat's litter box is cleaned out regularly.

3. Taking a dog out for some exercise.
4. Making sure the pet does not destroy the house, doesn't run (or fly) away, and stays out of trouble.

In this chapter, we concentrate on dogs and cats. Despite what you read about potbellied pigs, pet tigers, and other highly exotic animals, the most common job you'll get, by far, will be caring for a couple of the more than 180 million dogs and cats who currently call our homes their homes. Eva and Dorothy of New York say that although they care for all kinds of pets, their most frequent requests are for dogs and cats. Even if other animals such as birds, fish, or hamsters are in the mix, Fido and Fluffy will almost definitely be the basis for your pet-sitting visits. You'll find some specific information on other common house pets in Chapter 9, livestock and barn animals in Chapter 10, and more "exotic" pets in Chapter 11.

The Real Goal

Pet-sitting is appealing to owners because it means their pets are able to stay in their home environment. Although the pet's owner is not around, the pet is likely to feel more secure in familiar surroundings than in a kennel where their environment is disrupted and unfamiliar. While this is more important for some pets than others, most pets appreciate being in their home territory.

With that as the main criterion for hiring a pet-sitter in the first place, it is important for you to maintain as close to a normal routine as possible for the pets under your care.

You may want to segment your fees into half-hour time slots, but often a half hour is too short and an hour is too long for a home visit for the basic one-dog or one-cat pet-sitting scenario. Forty-five minutes seems to be a good amount of time to spend with the pet and then do some cleanup (scooping litter box, shaking dog blankets, etc.) while the pets eat. Then one last "walk" before you go. And, of course, a pat on the head and a smooch!

You also need to consider the time it takes to get to the job and back. This is discussed later in the chapter, but you will want to come up with a distance range that is included in your fee, and then any mileage beyond that is a surcharge. In some cases, the potential customer is simply out of your market range and you can't take on that customer at all.

Make a mental note on how far you can expand your territory, or even use Google Maps to help. Then focus on the essentials of the job, which starts with keeping pets well-fed.

Feeding

One of the most important services a pet-sitter provides is making sure the pet is fed. Again, being able to feed according to the pet's normal schedule is ideal.

Expect the owners to provide the food. In case they don't leave enough, be sure to have the owners write down what brand and type of food the animal eats (see Chapter 2 on setting up forms for basic information gathering). No animal should be abruptly changed to a different food at any time, least of all when they are under the stress of their owner being away.

Having the owner write down the type of food may seem unnecessary—if you empty the bag, you can just read the bag to see what kind of food the pet eats. However, many owners transfer their pet's food from a bag that you tear open on the top to a resealable container to retain freshness and keep pests out. You may reach the bottom of the container and find that the bag is nowhere to be found! Also, if the food is somewhat unusual and not readily found at the grocery store, be sure to have the owners write down where they purchase the food. When it comes to pet-sitting, you want to do your best to avoid surprises.

In Chapter 2 you learned about making a file for each of your clients and each of their pets. Write feeding information in your file, but be sure to check with each client every few weeks to see if the pet still eats the same amount and type of food. Dogs have been known to develop allergic reactions to foods over time, and veterinarians sometimes recommend starting the dog on a new type of food, which may have happened since your last job with this client. Also, these days, pets go on and off diets almost as often as people, so the quantity of food may have changed since you last sat for the pet.

Details, Details

Also be sure the owners tell you where you can find can openers, plastic can lids to cover unused portions of canned food, scissors for opening bags, and anything else they use on a daily basis to feed their pet.

Make sure to ask about idiosyncrasies. "Does Fido like water in his dry food?" "Does Fluffy like her canned food mixed in with her dry food, or does she like them served separately?"

Questions like these can mean the difference between Fluffy eating or going on a hunger strike while her owner is gone. A simple thing like where the animal normally eats can be an issue. Many herding dogs—such as border collies and shelties—are very sensitive to noise and vibration. If you put my border collie's food dish next to the refrigerator instead of by the back door, she may not go near it at all simply because it is in a different place, depending on how hungry she is. But she definitely won't eat if the refrigerator is running!

One of the main points of hiring a pet-sitter as opposed to depositing the pet at a kennel is to simulate the pet's common routine, so you need to know that routine.

Multiple Priorities

The placement of food dishes and which dish goes where on the floor first can be especially significant when you are sitting for more than one pet. Two dogs have a definite pack hierarchy. If they eat the exact same food, serving order can be less important—whichever bowl of food hits the ground first is the one the top dog will be eating.

However, if you are feeding two dogs two different foods or you are feeding a dog and cat, bowl placement can be critical. Some dogs never touch the family cat's food, although I have never owned one of those polite creatures. Cats rarely consume all their food in one sitting, so you may find you are feeding the cat on top of the washing machine in the laundry room (which also wouldn't stop our Labrador retriever . . .).

Be sure the owner gives you a rundown of the routine, and if you aren't provided with a detailed list, take some notes yourself.

Water, Water Everywhere

Do not forget water, an extremely important part of the feeding routine. There is not a pet on the planet who doesn't need 24-hour access to water. You cannot leave enough water. For example, put down two bowls for the dog or cat in case they spill one or something unpalatable drops in one. For a hamster, you would attach two tubes of water to the hamster cage just in case one loses its vacuum and all the water leaks out. And change their water after every feeding. Be sure to ask the owner approximately how much water the pet normally drinks in the course of a day. This way you are not only sure to leave enough water for the pet, but you also get a sense of whether the pet is consuming normal amounts of water, which may indicate a health issue that needs attention if they aren't.

Cats need their own water. Although most house cats that share the home with a dog will also drink out of the same water bowl, leave a water bowl specifically for the cat in the cat's eating area. Again, know the routine as the pet owners have set it up. Pets are familiar with the routine—when they eat and drink and where they eat and drink—so stick to the plan.

Doing Business

Another key job for the pet-sitter is to be sure the pet gets a chance to do his business on a regular basis. Dogs need to be walked several times a day—make sure the owner tells you their schedule. Cats typically just use a litter box. But the litter box needs to be changed regularly for the cat to be happy about using it. It doesn't hurt to have two litter boxes available to ensure they stay relatively clean. However, many cats are very particular about the kind of litter box they use, so if the owner doesn't have two, you may not want to purchase every different kind yourself just to have the right one to leave as a backup.

Because of the litter box issue and because cats can be left large amounts of food, which they eat only when hungry (unlike dogs who tend to eat all that is put in front of them), cats can often be visited just once a day to fill up the food dish, change the litter box, and check on the animal. The downside of this is that when cats are the sole house pet, owners often don't use pet-sitters for their care. For short periods, cats don't need any attention, and for longer periods, like a few days, cats can be easily tended by the friendly neighbor. You might gain some cat-only clients by suggesting in your marketing and advertising materials that even though cats can be self-sufficient, it is important for someone to check on the cat to make sure they are OK and not sick, injured, or stuck in the laundry chute. Cats also have very different personalities, and some of them like to cuddle with someone and/or enjoy being pet and even brushed. You can provide such care and offer to spend 45 minutes a day with Fluffy. Despite their reputation for being aloof, most house cats like having people around.

Dogs, on the other hand, need at least two outings a day, preferably more; and old dogs or puppies definitely need more. Although I don't know of a dog who has been trained to use a litter box, I'm sure it has happened. But don't expect it to have happened with one of your clients' dogs; it probably hasn't. If the dog is likely to have an accident even with two visits a day, consider using "training pads," which you can find in any pet supply store or large pet section in a department store or order online at www.petco.com. As long as the dog isn't inclined to chew the pads, they can make the dog more comfortable and make clean up so much easier. If the dog is going too frequently or not very often, let the owner know.

Be sure to find out from the owner what the dog's usual schedule is and where they are typically walked. Most dogs urinate almost every time they go outside, so that is easy. But, as with the old saying "a watched pot never boils," dogs seem not to defecate if you are eager for them to hurry up. If you know the dog's schedule, you are better able to time your visits accordingly. Also be mindful of the cleanup or pooper-scooper laws in most counties and follow them. Not doing so can cause problems for the dog's owners with their neighbors.

Some dogs are in an environment where you can feed and put them out in a secure pen in the morning, and then feed and bring them in when you do your evening visit—and they have had all day to take care of their business. It really depends on what the client's home setup is and what they are comfortable with.

In the wake of highly publicized pet kidnappings and theft of purebred animals, many pet owners are not willing to leave their dogs out all day unattended. If it is a close neighborhood with a neighbor who is home all day, the pet owner may be more comfortable with that. But in such a situation, the owner might just hire the neighbor to take care of the pet instead of hiring you. In other words, be prepared as a pet-sitter to get the more difficult jobs, not the easy ones!

Exercise

Most dogs need some daily exercise. Small dogs can get exercise just chasing a ball down the hallway. But even those easily entertained pups need to see the sunshine and get some fresh air every day, so dog owners probably want their dogs exercised at least once a day. Some dogs can be easily exercised by throwing a ball or a frisbee in the backyard, but others may need a vigorous half-hour walk to chill them out for the evening.

Try to do all off-the-leash exercise in a fenced area. If a fenced area is not easily available, get the owner's take on how best to exercise the dog. One option is to use an extra-long (30-foot) line for exercising horses to keep the dog attached to you while throwing a ball or frisbee disc to reduce the danger of the dog running away.

Get the Lowdown

You'll want to find out these things from your client before taking Rover out for a walk:

- ▶ Does Rover tend to get along with other dogs?
- ▶ On what route do you normally take Rover for a walk?
- ▶ Is there a house along that route that has a loose dog I should be aware of?
- ▶ If it is winter, windy, or rainy, does Rover normally wear a coat? Where is it?
- ▶ Do you typically use a choke collar, harness, or some other equipment when you walk Rover?
- ▶ Is there a fenced-in place where Rover could spend a few minutes off the leash safely?
- ▶ Is there a park or dog park you visit?
- ▶ Do you bring along treats to reward Rover for obedience on the walk? (This may be especially important if Rover is a puppy.)

Cat Exercise

"Cat" and "exercise" aren't words that are put together very often. Cats seem to need very little in the way of directed exercise. Cats seem to be quite capable of providing for themselves any exercise they need to stay healthy—such as following the sun around the house by walking from the upstairs bed to the downstairs sofa. Running and hiding in the closet when the pet-sitter comes seems to be another common cat exercise.

Cats do like to play, even well into adulthood. They don't seem to do this as much for exercise as for entertainment. Taking a few minutes to dangle a stuffed mouse on a string or roll a ball with a bell in it can bring a cat a day's worth of joy.

Laundry Time

Depending on the length of time the owner is away, you may need to clean or change the pet's bedding—wash dog beds or cat beds, or put fresh shavings in the hamster cage. Find out if it is OK to use the family washing machine for cleaning bedding—if one is in the home—but never leave it running when you leave. Preferably the client will leave an extra change of bedding, so you can put clean bedding on the dog/cat beds while you take the dirty ones to the laundromat (for a fee). This may include not just the specific dog and cat beds, but also blankets and towels left on human beds and chairs. Pets shed, and often almost as much cat or dog hair is on a pillow or towel is on the animal. You can also offer to take these items to the laundromat or run a load of laundry in their home as necessary.

Besides cats and dogs, other animals need cage cleanings and perhaps some "out" time. Birds may need to stretch their wings a little; rabbits may be accustomed to the run of the kitchen for 15 minutes every day. Some rabbits have an outdoor cage for some daily fresh air and sunshine. Because the main purpose of using a pet-sitter is to give the pet the closest to their usual day as possible, you are expected to fill in for everything the owner typically does with or for the pet.

Grooming

Significant grooming is covered under "added services." Your basic service should include everything the owner does on a daily or several-times-weekly basis. For example, your

---

tip

Cats don't typically like leashes. Don't attempt to walk a cat on a leash unless the owner informs you that the cat has been trained to a leash. Unlike dogs, leash walking does not seem to be as instinctive to cats as to dogs, and you could have quite a tangled mess on your hands. And if the cat gets really scared, you could have a much more dangerous situation with a cat that gets frightened, bolts, and is now running around loose or stuck at the top of a tree.

basic service does not need to include nail clipping for dogs—this task is commonly done once every three or four weeks, so unless the owner is gone for a month, this should not have to be your task (although you most definitely want to offer it as a service for an extra fee). However, if the dog or cat is long-haired and the owner tends to give the pet a quick brushing daily or every couple of days, you definitely will perform that task as part of your service. This is where it becomes wise to charge by the hour or set different rates for what you do on a visit. You will get an idea of how long it takes to do the basic pet-sitting service—feed, walk, change litter box—and that is your "basic" visit. Anything that takes you more than that half hour or hour warrants an

tip

Give your clients a menu of services that you are willing to perform over and above the basic ones relating to the pet. Then let them pick three that are most useful to them and include these in your basic charge. Any others on the list that they choose can be charged at an add-on rate.

extra fee. Anything that makes use of your specific expertise and credentials should be accounted for as a separate expense.

In other words, anyone can run a brush through a dog's hair for three minutes. But if you are expected to groom the dog with special trimming of hair, trim nails on a dog who is difficult about it, or brush a dog's teeth, these should be considered extras and need to be charged separately.

In a later chapter we discuss these added services, but you need to determine what your basic services are to come up with a basic fee. Add-ons are obviously over and above the basic services and can be provided in a kind of *a la carte* menu format, especially depending on the type of pet.

The Environment

Some of your basic services need to take into account the pet owner's home environment. Does the large, three-year-old German shepherd need to be driven to the park three miles away to get a good romp? Can the 12-year-old Shetland sheepdog run around the owner's fenced yard for 15 minutes and be ready for a good night's sleep? Does the owner live in a condo and walk their Samoyed three times a day and expect you to do the same? Your basic service may not include three visits a day, but if it does, your fees should reflect that.

Add Services to Your Menu

You can make getting the mail, picking up the newspaper, and other simple house-sitting functions free add-ons. You can also expand on such things and add functions that clients may want you to do while they are away—perhaps over a long weekend skiing in the Rockies, on vacation for ten days, or for the week on a business trip. The idea is that your client sees your brochure at their veterinary clinic when they stop in to buy pet food. At first, they consider hiring you to come to their house twice a day while they are gone to tend to their two small dogs and feed their parakeet, but they can't quite commit to using your service. They've never used a pet-sitter before; they usually take Puff and Duff to the kennel. But the last time they were there, they got fleas. And it is a pain trying to fit in the time to run them to the kennel and pick them up between all that needs to be done to prepare for their business trip.

Your brochure says you also bring in the mail and newspaper and otherwise help make the home look occupied. That's the clincher. They can not only leave Puff and Duff in their home environment, but they can also take comfort in knowing that someone is stopping by their vacant home twice a day.

These little extras can bring you customers. Don't promise the moon—don't agree to bake cookies for the neighborhood fundraiser that the pet's owners will miss because they will be out of town, or shovel the whole driveway, or stay for the afternoon while the plumber works on the bathroom because the only appointment the owner could get was while they were away.

However, in a service business, the most important thing is filling hours by performing a service. This can also mean house-sitting, provided it doesn't interfere with your regular schedule or clients. If someone needs a house-sitter for a couple of nights because they want someone to make sure their home is safe, you can step up and charge accordingly. This will usually be someone for whom you've already worked as a pet-sitter, or possibly a referral from a client who thinks you are trustworthy and reliable. Get a list of the wants and needs of the client and always have their cell number at the ready if you need to call them in an emergency.

Setting Clear Rates for Your Services

Figuring out how much to charge for your services can be difficult. It seems like it should be as simple as figuring out how much time you will spend and figuring in some gas money.

That is the basic premise. You do need to receive an hourly rate, and you need to pay for your expenses. Unfortunately, some expenses are fixed no matter how many clients you have. Insurance, licenses, association memberships, web hosting, and vehicle maintenance all cost you money each year whether you have one client or 100. Your fees need to accommodate those expenses while not pricing yourself so high that you dissuade customers from hiring you.

The best way to gauge what you should charge is to look at what your competition charges.

So What Do You Charge?

Many factors go into deciding on your fees. The main consideration—location—means fees can be wildly different around the country. Look online for pet-sitters in your area and see what they charge—if it's not on their website or if you see their name on a flier or get their name from a friend, call and pretend to be a customer. You want to make money, but you can't charge significantly more than the local competition unless you offer significantly better services and have done the job for a while. Reputation and add-on services are how you raise your rates.

But logic dictates that if you are a pet-sitter in northern New Hampshire, your fee schedule will probably be a bit lower than in southern California. And if you are in a rural area anywhere, your fees probably need to be lower than in metropolitan areas where people are closer to higher-paying jobs and have come to expect things to cost more than in the country. Also, if you are located in a metro area, your own expenses will be higher.

Balancing Diverse Clients

It is key that you figure out how many clients you can reasonably handle. Break your clients down into basic categories, after which you can determine how many clients you can fit into your schedule. Consider these three types of clients:

Client Type 1: Day Care

Perhaps the least time-consuming visits are day-care dog clients. For example, owners who work long hours hire you to come by perhaps in the morning and late in the afternoon to let the dogs out and give them their evening meals. Even long-term cat-sitting can require only one quick visit a day to refill the food bowl, change the litter box, refresh the water, and make sure you get at least a glimpse of Fluffy to check that she seems well.

Client Type 2: Long-Weekenders

Other clients may be people who go away on long weekend vacations a half dozen times a year. They are the ones who would rather have Fido stay in his home where he is more comfortable. By hiring you to come to their homes, they can leave on their trip right from work on Friday and come back whenever they want without having to time their return to when the kennel is open to pick Fido up. In fact, you can use these benefits to promote your service and attract exactly this type of client.

Client Type 3: Business or Extended Vacation Travelers

Some of your clients will be businesspeople who are away on extended four- and five-day trips during the week. They may be called away on a business trip without a lot of notice. Or you may have clients who go on a couple of seven- to ten-day vacations once or twice a year. These clients should provide you with plenty of notice. Both the business traveler and the extended vacation traveler require similar amounts of time as well as result in similar revenue and expenses.

Opinions differ about how long a dog should be left on their own at home vs. going to a kennel. You may find that even your regular customers use a kennel for extended trips of more than four or five days. If you are willing to stay in your customer's home for a week to ten days, you may get these extended jobs more frequently. If so, you should make it clear to your client that you need to be able to leave to do your regular jobs while pet-sitting in their home. House-sitting can provide you with more things to do for the client, such as mowing the lawn or shoveling snow.

Finding the Perfect Client Mix

Unless you really plan to focus your business on one type of client, you want to have a mix of the three groups. A mix provides you with a reasonable cash flow and a reasonable variety. And they all won't need your services at once, so if you can keep a good mix, you can keep yourself in work much of the time.

The day-care clients consume the least amount of time overall, but by nature, they need attention every day. The long-weekenders need a significant amount of time over that long weekend, but they are customers only five or six times a year. Obviously, longer visits and overnighters can provide more income. It's a matter of trying to fill your schedule without overlapping.

Business travelers can be the most time consuming. Many businesspeople choose not to have a pet because of the unpredictability of their day. However, with the increased availability of pet-sitters, even businesspeople with very hectic schedules can have a pet in their lives. And these people often have the discretionary income to hire pet-sitters on a regular basis.

Not only do business clients require a bit of your time, but they probably also occasionally need you to be available at a moment's notice. That means that while they can be lucrative customers who need your services often and are willing to pay decently as well as pay a surcharge for last-minute service, you still can't take on too many of them. If your pet-sitting business is thriving, you simply won't have the time.

Your Salary Expectations

One way to look at pricing is to figure out how much you need or want to make for income.

You need to list all your regular expenses, adding in some margin for the unexpected, like 15 percent. Next start factoring how many hours, and at what rates, you must work to earn at least enough to cover your expenses, plus 15 percent. Then you need to add on your profits.

Rates vary widely for pet-sitting with daily visits averaging $15 per hour according to ZipRecruiter. This will depend largely on where clients are located and how often you need to visit. Your rate also might depend on how many animals you have to take care of and what other services you provide. Overnight stays typically range from $40 to $100 per night.

According to ZipRecruiter, as of September 28, 2021, the average annual pay for the Pet Sitting jobs category in the United States is $30,819 a year. If you take $31,000 as an example of a goal (which may or may not be feasible in your geographic area), that means making roughly $600 a week assuming 50 weeks plus vacation pay. Note: Always know someone who can fill in for you if you're going to be away or need a backup for any reason—otherwise clients may find someone to fill in who takes your job.

It's a good rule of thumb to estimate your weekly earnings and earnings per hour based on how many hours you work per week—including pet sitting as well as commuting and managing your business. Since you may only be doing the actual pet-sitting job for 20 hours a week (or 40 visits) and spending the other 15 hours on traveling to and from clients and running your business—which includes marketing and buying what you need—you would need to charge $15 per half-hour visit (not per hour)... $15 x 40 visits = $600.

See what rates work best in your area, and if the numbers fall short, introduce your additional services (grooming, exercising, training, etc.) to justify or add to your rates.

This can give you a good idea of your income and how to adjust as necessary. For example, if you have too many clients who are far away and causing you to do more driving and less pet-sitting, then you will need to seek out clients closer to your home.

Play with the numbers for calculating overnighters as well. Keep in mind that getting paid something for the time you sleep is a benefit (although you won't get the same hourly rate), and your only real sacrifice is not sleeping in your own bed.

The Numbers Can Tell a Lot

Once you break your information down in this way, you may discover you need to get more of one type of client or less of another. Or you may determine you should charge more for some clients who are taking a larger chunk of your time than you realized. Your choice of client, and doing overnights in particular, may be set in part by your home life, other job schedule, or school schedule. If you're taking classes at night, overnighters may not fit into your plans.

Working as a pet-sitter gives you the flexibility to set your own rates and make a schedule that fits your needs while bringing in an income. You may also adjust your rates as you go, raising them for squeezing someone in when you are especially busy, or giving discounts when business is slow and you want to build your base of regular clients. In the next chapter we will explore how to build your client base through marketing and promotion.

Putting Your Best Paw Forward

Pet-sitting, like many service businesses, relies on having a large stable of customers to be successful. Even if on average each customer hires you once a month for two days, you need many customers simultaneously to have a successful business. The good news is the overhead is low, and more customers do not mean much more overhead outlay, except perhaps gas to get to the customers' homes.

The definition of *marketing* is basically to get word of your services to the group of people, or demographic audience, most likely to hire you. For pet-sitting that means spreading the word to pet owners that you are available to take care of their pets.

How you do that in a local area is typically through three marketing vehicles:

1. The internet, including social media platforms like Facebook and Nextdoor, among others
2. Advertising, paid or free if you can get it
3. Distribution of print materials

Before we get into those specifics, let's talk a little about the concept of a customer base.

Building a Customer Base

To keep revenue flowing, you need a steady stream of customers. In the pet-sitting business, this means figuring out how often people may be likely to hire you and then, with that in mind, coming up with the size of the customer base you need to earn enough money to cover your expenses and provide a profit. We discussed the need to know your demographics back in Chapter 1. Once you have a rough idea of how many pet lovers are in your area, with jobs outside the home, you can buckle down and plan a marketing strategy. In this chapter, we'll take a closer look at how to find customers.

Finding Customers

The most common way you will find customers is by word-of-mouth. Start spreading the word through your family and friends, as well as neighbors, the folks in your yoga, Zumba,

---

▶ Go Where the Dogs Are

For pet-sitters whose clients are mostly dog owners, print up a simple flier on your computer, run off copies, and head to the nearby park or dog park where you typically see a lot of people walking their canines. Walking is good exercise, not only for dogs but also for people. You'll find people are often friendly while walking their dogs, so ask their name (the dog's that is), and strike up a conversation, then give them your flier or at least a business card. Remember to have your email, phone number, website, and perhaps your Facebook or Instagram page listed on your flier and business card. If you want to approach the same audience online, join local pet groups' social media pages and become a regular commenter. You can build trust and name recognition if you are part of the community.

cooking, or creative writing class, and local merchants you visit often. Even your doctor, dentist, or hair stylist may have a pet in need of care or know someone with a pet in need of care. If you are doing this as a part-time career, you may mention it at your full-time job, but be careful; you don't want to give the impression you aren't taking your regular job seriously . . . even if that's true. But building a customer base and keeping a steady stream of jobs will require broadcasting your services across a wider range than friends or even friends of friends.

The Marketing Plan

A marketing plan may be part of an overall business plan if you use one. The plan should provide a strategy, complete with listed action items, to direct you in your search for business. If done well, a marketing plan should help you navigate the larger marketplace and find clients in your specific market.

When building a marketing plan, you will want to consider the following:

▶ Online marketing
▶ Social media marketing
▶ Print marketing materials and a list of where such printed material will be distributed (pet owners in dog parks, veterinary offices, etc.)
▶ Paid advertising
▶ Well-timed press releases
▶ Vehicle signs
▶ Other marketing vehicles, such as volunteer work

Decide what use each marketing component will serve. Then decide when to use it. Set up a marketing calendar and follow it.

This should include:

▶ When to post on social media (hint: look for similar/competitive social accounts)
▶ When you need to get ads submitted (hint: only do inexpensive advertising in local papers and ask how much lead time they need prior to publication)
▶ When to do email blasts (only to people whose email you have attained with their permission— otherwise, it's spam)

tip

Amy C. of Amy's Animal Care in Maine has created an information packet she sends out to potential customers who call inquiring about her pet-care service. The packet includes her price list; information sheets on how to find a pet-sitter and how to help your pet-sitter give excellent care; and a bit of promotion on why you should hire her, including a business-card refrigerator magnet.

▶ When local events are happening where you can hand out fliers and/or business cards

Your Website and Online Marketing

Where do most people look for goods and services these days? On the internet. Therefore, you must have a website and social media presence. Your website should provide all sorts of information and added value to your business. However, for a localized service business such as pet-sitting, you don't need to go overboard with a web presence. The internet reaches billions of people, and your market area might just be a few thousand; you can see the logic of keeping your website small.

What can a local business use a website for? Potential customers often prefer to check out your website to see all the details about your business before picking up the phone and talking to you in person. Your well-designed website can spur customers to call and line you up for their next out-of-town trip.

Your website should, of course, include any and all information about what your pet-sitting service provides, why your services are so great, and other useful information that will pull them in. You should include:

▶ Contact information, such as your name, your phone number, your email address, and links to your Facebook page and any other social media accounts like Instagram or LinkedIn

▶ A bio about you, with an emphasis on dependability, and a very brief bio about any independent contractors you use (don't include their direct contact information; you don't want to potentially lose business directly to your contractors)

▶ A brief history of your business

▶ A menu of your services and a price list (if some prices will vary based on various factors, just say "ask about pricing" or put a price range)

▶ A list of the types of animals you will pet-sit

▶ Information page, detailing the pet-care services you provide

▶ Links to any veterinary clinics, groomers, pet supply stores, feed stores, and other businesses that refer clients to you

While the site should certainly be fun and attractive, don't make it too complicated. Keep the layout simple, and make it user-friendly—just one click to find whatever customers are looking for. Make sure your homepage contains all the basic information: if visitors to your site go no further than the homepage, they should be able to judge your style, learn your basic qualifications, and know how to reach you. Pet-sitting is an uncomplicated service business for the most part; you want to make it appear that way.

Don't forget the photos—people love photos, especially of pets. If you're posting any photos of pets you sit for or of your friend's dog, cat, or other animal, make sure it's OK with them—people are usually happy to see their pets online, but you should always ask.

One instance where you might want your website to get a little more complex is if you have expanded your business to include products you sell online and send through the mail. This will entail having a Shopping Cart on your site and being set up to take credit card payments or use PayPal. This depends on how aggressively you want to market that aspect of your business.

You can also include a blog on your site—pet related, of course. Blogs don't need to be more than two or three paragraphs, but if they are clever, informative, or include funny stories, people may return often. You can even include a survey, a quiz, or a contest with a minimal prize. This not only keeps people coming back, but it also captures their email addresses, which they'll need to include in case they win the prize. Building an email list is very important.

tip

Linking with other businesses' websites can increase your visibility. This is often set up as an exchange. They put a link to your site on their site; you link to their site on yours. And if at first that doesn't make sense, remember pet owners need health insurance, car repairs, and rug cleaning as well as things directly related to their pets!

If you find articles on other websites that you think would be of interest to your clients or potential clients, you can either paraphrase them or link viewers to the source of the article. You should also swap links with complementary businesses in your market area.

Always think of your website as a marketing tool to bring in customers. Its most important function may be just as a way for you to gain credibility, but that goes directly to bringing in customers.

Lastly, always be sure to keep your website updated. Nothing says "out of business" more than dated marketing materials or dead links that go nowhere. If you find you aren't able to keep the site up-to-date, you will want to reduce its presence to simply an attractive homepage that shows your pertinent contact information.

Email Marketing

You can use email marketing to get potential customers to opt in to receiving your newsletters. You can also use email addresses obtained from potential customers to send short emails with announcements, upcoming sales and discounts on services or products, news such as adding a new territory where your clients may have friends, or other informative items like what to do about pet allergies. Time your emails so they are not too frequent (once a week tops). According to a Direct Marketing Association survey, 35 percent of their marketers send two or three emails per month. Another 19 percent send just one email per month, while 9 percent send six to eight emails per month.

Have a place on your website and on your pet-sitting contract that gives customers the opportunity to receive your newsletter. Make it appealing—offer a discount or free (cheap) giveaway if they sign up. Always ask new clients for email addresses. Be sure to note on the form that you will not give your email address list out to other businesses so your customers can be assured they will get information only from you.

The key to a successful newsletter is to keep it simple—and useful. Provide your clients with important information regularly, including:

tip

If you like to write, are good with deadlines, and can fit in the time, approach a local website and offer a weekly blog, or go to a local weekly newspaper and ask about writing a pet-related column. This is a great way to get your business name in front of your target market on a regular basis. The column gives you automatic credibility that will give your potential customers one more reason to call you before looking elsewhere.

- ► *Ideas that can help with your care of their pets.* For example, a form they can print out and post near their phone listing all important phone numbers.
- ► *Pet-care tips.* Pet owners who are dedicated enough to hire a pet-sitter for their pets are also dedicated to providing quality care for their pets. Those owners will read just about anything to glean more information on how to take care of the animals sharing their home. Provide something of use in every newsletter—health-care tips, feeding information, grooming ideas, current research, etc.
- ► *Coupons from local merchants.* Merchants love simple ways to advertise their businesses, especially if you do it all for them. Offer to put a business-card-size ad in your newsletter in exchange for being able to offer your customers a discount or coupon to use at their business. Everyone wins this way—your customers get something of value, they think kindly of your business because you have offered them something of value, and the business owners gain new customers by getting people into their stores.

Collecting Email Addresses

You can use your website to collect email addresses, as mentioned earlier, with a contest or with a coupon. You'll also want to compile a local email list so you can send out an occasional email blast with a savings offer, a great pet photo, and/or a brief story. If people give you their email address, you can use it to reach out to them. If, however, you get their email through another source, such as a list they don't know they are on, people may consider your messages spam and not want to do business with you.

You can collect emails by attending local functions and networking or by having a booth at a local fair or carnival. If you offer something, such as a prize, a freebie, or a special discount, people will sign up—all you need is their name and email address. This is so important if you also sell pet-friendly items.

Anytime you can add email addresses to your list, do so. But use email judiciously—if you email too often, people will simply delete your emails or block you. Reach out every couple of weeks to your email list with something of interest, and don't forget to send cute photos. Don't send attachments—people are leery of opening them.

Social Media

It's hard to find anyone who does not have a social media presence. Even if you don't engage often, you should have an Instagram and/or Facebook presence. Instagram is photo-oriented, and what better photos to post than pet photos? Facebook puts you in touch with tons of people, many of whom are pet owners. Local social media like Nextdoor is another opportunity to touch base with customers in your area—and those are the customers you're looking to reach.

Also look for local social media pages that focus on your neighborhood. Many towns, counties, and communities feature such local social media sites. Don't just advertise and promote; start conversations about pets, answer people's questions, post some cool facts, and be part of the discussion. That's how social media works. Let people know you're out there, and have them contact you rather than being pushy.

Printed Marketing Materials

Every business owner needs a business card. You can also benefit from marketing materials such as brochures and fliers. Here are the usual suspects and how you can use these and other materials specifically in the pet-sitting biz.

Business Cards

A number of business card software programs are available for your computer, whether you have a PC or a Mac. Programs like Design & Print or Business Card Factory can be had for less than $30, and you can print numerous cards.

Many business card software packages include copyright-free clip art that allows you to jazz up your business card with pet-related graphics and photos. You can even scan a photo of you and your pet or pets and then drop it into place on your business card—a personal touch that conveys a great message about your knowledge and love of animals.

Even if you want to have the local copy shop or an office supply store create your business card for you, it is not a huge expense. And these places have a larger array of logos, graphics, and fonts for you to choose from than your basic desktop software offers.

You can also order business cards online from places like www.moo.com, www.vistaprint.com, or www.gotprint.com. You can design the card on their website and order a ton of cards for a reasonable price. It's very simple.

Be sure to design your card to reflect the kind of business you have. If your pet-sitting service does not include large animals, do not use a horse for a logo. This is simply misleading and confusing. On the other hand, you don't have to include a photo or graphic of every kind of pet you are willing to care for. Your business card can hold a fair number of words to explain your service. For instance, Tanya K., a pet-sitter in New Hampshire, has almost 60 words on her business card! Not only is it still highly readable, but the card covers a great amount of information about her service and her credentials. Tanya's card, which is shown in Figure 4.1 on page 53, includes her business name, phone number, and email address.

That's a huge amount of information for a business card, and she includes four pictures to boot! It's all on a coated card with a light-blue background, an easy-to-read typeface, tons of information, lots of style, and the extra cute factor. This one stands out in a crowd.

Business cards need not be that complex; they are small by nature. A dog or cat graphic can provide the most immediate representation of your business, but if you are willing to provide pet-sitting for almost any type of animal, include a line that gets that across. "Any type of house pet welcome" or some other simple wording conveys that you don't provide care for barn animals, but you would sit for an iguana. You could also say "no exotic animals" or "some exotic animals" to draw the attention of someone who owns a ferret.

Unless you have a physical office, you won't need to put your address on the card. But do be sure to include all contact information, including your email, website, Facebook and/or Instagram page, and cell phone number.

Time for Pets

Dependable, Friendly Care

at Your Home or Barn

While You Are Working or Vacationing

Pet-sitting services include daily visit(s) with playtime

Exercise, feeding, trips to groomer or veterinarian

Barn care including stalls, feeding, grooming, turnout, and more!

Fully insured

Red Cross certified in pet first aid

Call for a Free Consultation

222-333-4444 or email TimeforPets@abc.com

FIGURE 4–1: **Sample Business Card**

Having business cards in your wallet or in a special holder is one thing, but you need to get in the habit of handing out a business card to everyone you meet. With more than half of American households having pets, it is a good bet that whomever you give a business card to may be a prospective client. You may even ask people if they know other pet owners and if you can give them a couple of cards to share with their friends.

Business cards are also handy for posting on bulletin boards because they take up little space and will be more likely to be left up for the long term. And they make easy and inexpensive ads because many publications offer a "business card section" for advertising. You can create a professional-looking business card in literally minutes, or order cards and have them delivered in a very short time; you have no reason not to have a supply of business cards on hand at all times.

Brochures

Trifold brochures also can be easily designed and printed on your home computer. This is where you can provide lots of information to prospective clients about you and your services. Have these brochures ready for any local chamber of commerce event you attend, and for bringing to trade shows, dog shows, or any other venue where pet owners gather. Some veterinarians will let you leave a stack in their waiting area, depending on how much

► Slogans

We'd like to interrupt this discussion on print materials for a brief word on slogans. A marketing slogan can help garner attention. You could spend a lot of money and hire someone who has marketing experience to come up with your slogan, but that seems best left for Coca-Cola and other multibillion-dollar international companies. For a small business, no one can come up with a more perfect slogan than you.

That's not to say you can't solicit ideas from friends and relatives. In fact, you could have a pizza party with the specific intention of bantering slogan ideas around for your new business.

You'll notice that Tanya K., pet-sitter from New Hampshire, uses a simple slogan on her business card shown on page 53: "Dependable, friendly care." That's about the most important information a pet-sitter's potential clients will want to know.

When you come up with your slogan, use it everywhere—on your business card, on your website, on your brochures, in your phone messages, and even at the top of your invoices.

room they have. Use your brochures in displays like those local banks often offer—local businesses with an account at the bank can sometimes have a display table for a week in the bank lobby.

Brochures are great tools for spelling out the details of your business, from your specific services to a price list. You can also create your brochure as a self-mailer. This way, when a prospective client calls and asks for information, your voice message can request they leave their address so you can add them to your mailing list. Then you can print out a label, stick it on your brochure, and mail it to the caller immediately.

Mailing brochures can provide an excellent marketing tool that can make the difference between gaining a new client or not.

Some of the things you want to cover in a brochure are:

► An overview of your business. Just a couple of paragraphs will do. Include when the business started and why.

► Your biography. Be sure to include why you chose this business. Feel free to talk about your own pets. In fact, make sure you do. Include a picture of you with your pets. Also talk about your business abilities and other background info that will build the trust and confidence prospective clients need to feel before they hire you.

► Your approach to health safety and protocol is important, such as having had COVID-19 vaccines and a policy of wearing a mask indoors if other people are around, unless they let you know that it is okay not to wear a mask. Include your COVID-19 protocol in your brochure.

▶ A list of services. What do you offer: in-home visits, feeding, exercising, grooming, litter box changing?

Fliers

Fliers are inexpensive to create on your computer. A single-sheet, small flier can be handed out to people that you meet or passersby. You can also post a flier on bulletin boards. Fliers like this are especially good for advertising an upcoming event you are holding or sponsoring, or for some special notice, such as a one-year anniversary special.

Include those convenient little tear-off strips on the bottom of the page so people can take your number with them. Make the strips wide enough that you can include a line like "pet-sitting service" or your company name, if it is self-evident what service you provide, above your number. People stuff those little strips deep into pockets—and they pull them out several days later when they are cleaning out their jeans pockets before sticking the pants in the wash. Chances are prospective customers won't remember what the number was for—but if you add your little tag line, they will do an "Oh yeah, this is that pet-sitting service that sounded perfect for when we go to Montreal for that long weekend in September." They just might give you a call or shoot you an email or text!

Be sure to freshen up your fliers on a regular basis. Just like an outdated website, nothing says "probably no longer in business" more than a flier that's dated, faded, ripped, curled, and rained on. If the flier looks old, potential customers may think you haven't been around to change it because you are no longer pet-sitting.

tip

Paid advertising can be a money sucker. Good ad salespeople can make you think that if you advertise in their newspaper or magazine, your sales will skyrocket. If you decide to spend money on paid ads, be sure to use a method that helps you track response. Coupons that follow the model of "Clip this ad and receive a free gift" or other specials related only to that specific ad are good ways to see how many customers an ad generates.

Paid Advertising

In this business, the amount of advertising you need depends on how many clients you are willing and able to take on. If you're using social media to get your name out there and are well-connected among the local pet owner and pet business communities, you will probably get all the clients you need from word-of-mouth and never need to spend a penny paying for ads. You can also get listed in local online directories; many are free.

However, if you'd like to build a bigger client base, paid advertising options to consider include:

▶ *Circulars.* You could ask a pet store, even if it's a chain, if you could produce a card and pay to have the card inserted into their circulars for a certain distribution area. This is called a blow-in card. These fliers are usually easily sorted by ZIP code.

▶ *Pet-related newsletters.* Local animal shelters typically publish a newsletter to send to all contributing members. Ads are typically inexpensive for a yearlong contract.

▶ *Newspapers.* Often, newspaper ads will be prohibitively expensive, depending on the circulation of the paper in your area. But most newspapers recognize the value of providing an opportunity for small businesses to advertise in their papers and create specific small-business ad pages. These often consist of business-card-size classified ads that are very reasonable in price, especially if you can spring for ongoing placement.

▶ *Classified magazines.* Another advertising vehicle that is within the budget of a small business is the classified magazine. These usually offer commercial listings at rates that are higher (but still reasonable) than the personal listings the magazines mostly contain. Some magazines also have display ads. Just be sure the publication's distribution area stays mainly within the service range of your business.

▶ *Paid online advertising.* There are several options that you can explore when entering the world of online paid advertising. Social media sites are the popular places to be seen; pay-per-click ads are also an option as are ads on appropriate websites frequented by pet owners. The issue is a need for local advertising—since pet care is usually a local business. If the web hosting service or website lets you narrow down your reach by specifying certain areas in which you want the ad to run, you can save yourself a lot of money—after all, if you are in Pennsylvania and you put an ad on GoogleAds, you may get a bloke clicking on your ad from Australia looking for someone to walk his kangaroo. As much fun as that sounds, you should think only about ads you set up to run locally or look at local sites. Pay-per-click can also add up very quickly—put maximums on daily clicks, and keep a close eye on your advertising costs.

Well-Timed Press Releases

A press release can be a simple avenue to free publicity. Send a press release announcing the opening of your business to every local newspaper in your market range as well as local websites. Get the names of editors or a webmaster, and email it to their attention. Send it to several editors—the business editor, the lifestyle editor, the Sunday edition editor, and the news desk. This may get you an interview and an article on your startup business in at least one of the papers. But don't just send an announcement that you are starting a business—many businesses start each week, so it's unlikely you're going to get a story based on that alone. Instead, be the first to provide your particular pet service in your area. What can you offer that is newsworthy? Or perhaps it's about a benefit to the community. For example: New pet-sitting service offers three free days of pet-sitting to all U.S. military veterans or active members of the armed forces. If you want to stand out among the 25 other new businesses looking for attention and free publicity, give them a reason to focus on you and your business.

Press releases can be great publicity generators at other pertinent times, too. Here are some ideas:

- ▶ About a month before school vacations, send out a press release talking about the importance of remembering to line up care for Fido during the busy vacation season.
- ▶ Keep tabs on research, and when a new report comes out, send out an information sheet describing the health benefits of keeping Fido fit and trim, and discuss what your service offers to help keep dogs exercised.
- ▶ Send out information tips about pre-flea-season pest control or how to keep your pets safe during the hectic holidays. This will establish you as a pet expert and get your business name out there.

The point is to think of something to say that will benefit the readers of the publication, or website. Think "them" instead of "you," and you'll have some good press releases. To learn more about press releases go to www.pressreleases.com and click on PR Writing, or Google "writing press releases," and you'll find a number of articles.

Vehicle Sign

This is a tricky one. The value of having a magnetic sign on the door of your vehicle is great—with pet-sitting, you do a lot of driving around and lots of people will see your ad. But make sure to take the sign off your vehicle when parked in someone's driveway, so it doesn't call attention to the fact that when you leave, the house will be vacant.

One other consideration is insurance. The difference between having a personal automobile insurance policy and being required to purchase a commercial policy may be as simple as whether there is signage on the vehicle. (See Chapter 6 for more information on insurance.)

Association Memberships

Membership in local associations—the chamber of commerce, a pet-sitters' organization, a veterinary-related group—not only provides you with some great ideas and moral support, but also customers. Bring a stack of business cards to chamber of commerce meetings, and don't leave until you've handed out most of them. Remember, pets are part of more than half of all American households, so don't assume someone is not a potential customer or a potential referral just because their business isn't pet related. If they don't have pets themselves, their relatives, friends, acquaintances, and employees do!

Be judicious in your membership in national associations. While dues are typically modest, be sure the association is worth all the extra mail, and probably email, you will receive. It won't take long for you to realize that the schedule of a pet-sitter doesn't allow for much active participation in associations. But many offer beneficial services, such as your name on a list on their website where people can search for pet-sitters by region.

Likewise, get your website linked on other sites. Think broadly when it comes to websites of businesses within your market area. Again, the business itself may not be pet related, but many of the workers at the business may own pets. You would be best to limit this kind of marketing to those businesses that hire professionals who make a high enough salary to afford pet-sitting services. Think of businesses that have employees such as salespeople and lecturers who are on the road a lot and potentially in need of someone to care for their pets regularly.

You should become a member of your nearest chamber of commerce (COC). If you are in a very small town, you may need to join the COC in the nearest "city." Of course, you'll want to be sure it is in your market range because one thing you will get out of the COC is potential customers; you don't want them to be so far away that you have to spend all your earnings in gas just to get there.

In addition to the benefits you get from being a COC member, your association is one more way to show the world you are a professional and you understand being businesslike is important no matter what business you are in.

Speak!

Giving seminars on pet care or speaking at local pet club gatherings can be time consuming, but it is a very focused way of marketing yourself and your services. You will be speaking directly to groups of people who are your target market: pet owners. Pet people hang with other pet people, so the net you cast is much wider than just the group of people sitting in front of you.

Being a speaker and offering seminars also gives you additional credibility that you can add to your list of impressive credits—you are knowledgeable enough about pets and pet care to speak about your expertise to others. Be sure to get a press release out about any speaking engagements you are lined up for—it is a great opportunity to get your business mentioned in the newspaper or on a pet-related website.

tip

If you see a diner in your area that has advertising on their place mats, call the number and see about the pricing. Putting your information and a great pet picture on place mats is usually a cheap means of advertising. Local church bulletins are also an inexpensive way to get the word out to your immediate community.

Offer to speak to a group at the local animal shelter—perhaps with the marketing pitch that if people are hesitant to adopt that pet they've always wanted because they are worried about how to care for the pet when they have to go away, you can offer some tips. Have a handout available to which you can staple your business card, so people at the seminar not only have your name and number on the handout but they can pass your business card along to a friend or colleague.

Start small on the speaking circuit and build to larger audiences if it interests you. But be sparing in your speaking engagements—you'll want to stick to your target market area if it is to be beneficial to you, and you don't want to wear out your audience! Hint: Speaking isn't as easy as it looks. Prepare and time out your speech—make it interesting and entertaining, and practice, practice, practice. Yes, it's time consuming, so make sure it's worth the effort.

Try Something Different

People with pets are found in all sorts of places. Not only do they buy pet food at the pet store and bring their pet to the veterinarian, but they also go to the dentist, the library, and the grocery store. Just as with website link exchanges, think outside the box when it comes to where you post your pet-sitting signs.

The rule of thumb is people need to see and hear things three times to really register and remember the message. If a pet owner sees your flier at the grocery store Saturday, then again at the local convenience store Wednesday evening when they stop for the paper on their way home from work, then three weeks later they decide to go away for a long weekend and they ask their veterinarian for the name of a trustworthy pet-sitter, and your name comes up, the potential client will think: "Oh yeah, I've seen postings for Any Pet, Any Time pet-sitters in a couple of places now. They seem to be very businesslike, getting their name out there. And my vet recommends them, so I'll give them a call." And just like that, you have a new client.

Useful Credentials

Small-business owners often have to be the proverbial "jack of all trades." Fix the computer printer, make the coffee, do the bookkeeping, and perform the actual business of the business! In any small business, the business owner has an equation to balance.

One side of the equation is your knowledge of your specific business—in this case, animals. Do you know how to feed animals? Are you knowledgeable enough about their health to know when something is wrong? Do you know how to interact with the types of animals that will be under your care?

The other side of the equation is your business knowledge. Managing your finances, bookkeeping, and marketing are the most important business aspects you will need to know.

When starting out, you may want to learn how to write a concise business plan, particularly if you are looking for funding. You will also need to know how to present yourself in a businesslike manner to your clients.

For pet owners to want to hire you to take care of their pets, the main thing they want to know is that you are dependable. You will need references and referral sources who attest to your reliability, trustworthiness, and responsibility. These references need to be professionals and "publicly known" people such as veterinarians, community leaders, etc., not your personal family and friends who would probably be completely unknown to the potential client. (That being said, if you and your prospective customer have a friend in common who will give you a good reference, you should consider that to be a legitimate name to provide.) You also want to enhance your resume with certifications and licenses, which we'll talk about later in this chapter. But probably more important than any piece of paper, your potential clients want to know you have experience with pets.

Firsthand Experience

The best way to have experience with pets is to have pets of your own. Flaunt it if you do. Instead of a little cartoon animal on your business card, include a nice photo of you and your happy pets. No more fundamental credential for a pet-sitter exists than being a pet owner whose pets seem content and well cared for.

Having pets of your own means you know how important it is to pet owners that their animals are taken care of properly. When you take on pets, you take on the responsibility of taking care of their needs because they cannot do this for themselves. When you bring pets into your house, they cannot go foraging for food and find water; you have to provide it for them. Pets cannot let themselves out to relieve themselves; you need to make sure they are let out on a regular schedule. And pet owners relinquish that responsibility to you, the pet-sitter, when they leave their pets in your care.

If you don't have pets, don't advertise that fact. You must have great affection for animals to be successful in the pet-sitting business. Chances are if you are considering this line of work, you do like animals, so prepare yourself with a satisfying answer when your potential client asks you if you have pets. Is your apartment too small? Does your landlord not allow pets? Perhaps you are grieving a pet you recently lost and aren't ready for another. Are you getting into the pet-sitting business specifically because you love animals but can't have pets of your own at the moment, so you are vicariously having pets through your clients? Whatever you do, don't tell a prospective customer that you don't have pets because they are too much of a pain to care for. That will turn off any self-respecting pet owner. And if this is how you really feel, pet-sitting probably isn't the best job for you.

Training

Have you taken obedience training classes, perhaps just to educate your own pets? Dog training classes can be not only a great credential for a pet-sitter but also a potential add-on service (see Chapter 12 for more on expanding your business). Dog owners will be happy that you know enough to not allow Fido to jump all over you when you come to care for him—something they may have been trying to teach the dog for months, so if you let him jump, you greatly set back their training.

Or perhaps the owners have been trying unsuccessfully to teach Fido not to jump and will pay you extra to work on this problem with him when you visit. This lets you raise your fee. So when you enroll in an obedience training class, it may well pay for itself in just a couple of jobs. Google such classes in your area and sign up. Keep in mind that while no specific licenses are required to become a pet-sitter, learning appropriate skills and even having some credentials that enhance your appeal can help you land potential clients.

However, don't promote yourself as a dog trainer if you have done nothing more than teach your own dog to sit or taken a couple of classes. Dog training requires expertise and experience. If you make it clear you are not an experienced dog trainer, but you would be happy to help Fido learn not to jump, you can still charge a fee for an extra half hour of your time. But keep in mind that all the training in the world does not help if the owners aren't willing to learn to do the same things you do to help Fido understand that jumping is unacceptable.

Best in Show

Another feather in your cap could be if you enter your own dogs or cats in competitions. This doesn't mean simply show competitions where your pet mostly competes at looking like a classic example of the breed. Agility work—where dogs go through tunnels, jump over fences, and balance on teeter-totter-like boards at their owner's direction and under time pressure—has become huge in the U.S. And working-dog competitions involving border collies or other stock dogs bred to work with livestock are getting almost as popular in the U.S. as in the United Kingdom and Australia.

If you do this kind of work with your pet, you get two benefits. Your clients know you are a serious pet owner because having an animal that competes takes commitment to the animal's optimal health and training. Also, at a competition, you are among many other pet owners who may be able to shuffle some clients your way!

Of course, it would be difficult to do any serious level of competition while establishing a pet-sitting business—a lot of the competitions take place on the weekends, which, of course, are exactly when you will be most wanted for your pet-sitting jobs. But if you are still in the business-planning stages, you might consider adding something like competition to your resume, or if you have competed in the past, make sure to promote that! Having success at a competition is a better credential than if you and your pet never placed, but even if you didn't, the experience of competing brings a certain level of pet knowledge. This shows your ability to work closely with animals, teach obedience, and see results.

Grooming

Do you love grooming dogs and cats? Even if you don't want to offer this service to your clients, knowing that you have the skill or some training in it lets pet owners know you have experience with animals. That experience isn't restricted just to grooming. To groom a pet, you need to know how to handle the animal. That kind of hands-on experience can be valuable to pet owners. It shows your comfort level and ability to remain in control while taking care of an animal.

You may not want to go into full-fledged grooming services, but you can offer some of the simple things, such as basic brushing, nail trimming, and cleaning of ears.

Refer to Chapter 12 on expanding your business for further details on serious grooming services and what you need to get started. A real boon to a service like grooming is it leads you to pet-sitting clients and vice versa.

First Aid Training

The American Red Cross offers a training program for pet first aid. While directed toward the pet owner, this training program is perfect for a pet-sitter and offers additional peace of mind to pet owners who hire you.

The program teaches students how to react in a number of emergencies, including choking, bone fractures, being hit by a car, and natural disasters. It teaches CPR and covers basic health parameters for dogs and cats, some bird information, and even some tips on other small mammals and reptiles, all of which you may find under your care.

Check with your local Red Cross chapter for a pet first aid training program near you. The Red Cross also offers a pet first aid book and an instructional video by the Greater Los Angeles Chapter. The American Red Cross website includes helpful information at www.redcross.org.

If you take Red Cross pet first aid training, make sure to add that info to any marketing you do for your pet-sitting service.

Be a Techie

With the explosion of pet ownership has come an explosion in the need for veterinary services. And for every veterinary clinic, several technicians are needed. To fill this need, veterinary technician programs are springing up all over the country. As of this writing, their student numbers are growing by leaps and bounds.

Pet owners are spending more than ever before on their pets, from basic veterinary care to high-quality food to surgery and treatment of serious conditions that may include expensive medication. Technicians play no small part in the overall pet-care picture.

Amy C., a pet-sitter from Maine, is a licensed veterinary technician (LVT). She spent time as a practicing LVT in a veterinary clinic. This added considerably to her credentials. In fact, it was the requests she got to pet-sit from customers when she worked at the clinic that made her think about going into the business in the first place. The clinic became a great source of client referrals. "Being a vet tech means a lot to people," Amy says she has found.

Licensed veterinary technicians go through a two-year training program in which they learn how to give shots, provide emergency first aid, observe and recognize diseases, draw blood, perform routine dental care, collect lab samples, etc. Although the amount of education required is less than in human nursing, vet techs are the registered nurses of the pet world. They cannot offer diagnoses, perform surgery, prescribe medications, or give a prognosis. That leaves a lot left to do. Most of their activities are in the presence of a veterinarian. However, they can recognize the symptoms of an illness and provide input and recommendations to pet owners.

For those interested in specializing, programs are available beyond the two-year degree. However, for the purposes of running your own pet-sitting business, you probably don't need to get this far in depth (or in debt!). The specialties tend to be in areas such as radiography, anesthesia, orthopedics, and other medical-related topics you do not find much of a call for in the pet-sitting world.

With the veterinary technician credential comes great trust from clients. You can take on more complex situations, such as caring for pets who have had surgery and need day-to-day care in the home during their recovery—a licensed vet tech doing home care can offer

▶ **Learn From the Pros**

CPPS-Certified Professional Pet Sitter® is a federally trademarked certification mark PSI awards to professional pet-sitters who successfully demonstrate their knowledge and skills by obtaining a passing score on the CPPS exam and agree to adhere to PSI's Recommended Quality Standards and Code of Conduct and Ethics.

You can learn more at www.petsit.com/certification, or call (336) 983-9222.

a great amount of relief to the working pet owner. You can charge more for these services than for routine care. And you can feel a great sense of satisfaction from your work, which involves a lot more than simply making sure Fido does his business.

Even if you don't find much need (thankfully) for heavy-duty medical services, just knowing how to clip nails or administer medication, or simply having a general idea when something is wrong, boosts your credibility as a pet-sitter.

Visit Your Veterinarian

If you don't have the time, money, or inclination to go the licensed veterinary technician route, spend some time with your veterinarian. Most veterinarians are probably too busy to give away time; ask if you could pay a fee for a couple of appointment times and have the vet show you things like how to give different kinds of shots (subcutaneous—or under the skin—and intramuscular). Learn about good restraint practices for dogs and cats, emergency procedures, and administering pills. Your veterinarian can also give you a list of common diseases and conditions to watch for.

Don't keep this to yourself. While "spent an hour learning from my veterinarian" isn't something you would put on a flier, do mention it to prospective customers. Not only does it show you have learned specific techniques from a professional, but the fact you made the effort at all shows you are determined to give high-quality care to your customers.

Nutrition

You won't find any licensed credentials for pet nutrition. However, you can do many things to learn more about it.

Google "pet nutrition" and read up on all sorts of nutritional information, such as what a dog, cat, or bird needs for nutrition; specialized nutrition like vegetarian diets for pets; the use of raw meat; and the value of supplements. All the major pet food manufacturers

▶ Better Business Bureau (BBB)

The BBB is a watchdog organization with the consumer in mind. The BBB requires you be in business at least six months to join, and your business must meet its rigorous standards. The BBB is where customers register complaints, and the bureau will investigate those complaints and report on its findings. Anyone interested in doing business with you (or anyone at all, for that matter) can look at any complaint received by the BBB about your business and the BBB's findings.

Again, not a deciding factor in itself, but one more notch in your favor if your potential customers see you are a member of the BBB. Pet owners simply will not take chances with their pets.

The BBB offers comprehensive standards by which it feels businesses should abide. Some of these that relate to a service business such as pet-sitting are:

▶ Truthful, nondeceptive advertising.

▶ Price comparisons to identical products/services from competitors.

▶ Use of the word "free" only for giveaways that are unconditional.

▶ Disclosure of any extra charges.

▶ Ad designs that are clear to the customer and minimize the possibility of a customer misunderstanding the offer or message.

▶ Use of objective, not subjective, superlatives. For example, "the best" tends to be a subjective superlative because everyone's opinion of what is the best can be different. An objective superlative may be "the only pet-sitter who offers obedience training." The BBB expects you to be able to back up any such claims.

▶ Use of endorsements and testimonials should be actual and not fabricated, and should be used in the context in which the testimonial was given.

▶ Any claims of performance or quality of care should be backed up by data.

(Science Diet®, Iams®, and Purina®, for a short list) have websites with good information about nutrition in general and their products specifically.

Go to your local feed store and pick up literature on all the various pet feeds. (Bring your sport utility vehicle—many feed stores carry dozens of pet brands, each of which has dozens of varieties.)

Go to classes or seminars put on by local schools, pet-related stores, medical facilities, or shelters. If you live near a university with an equine studies program or a large animal hospital (that would be either a hospital for large animals or a large hospital for small animals), they often offer seminar series or workshops on animal nutrition. Also check with pet organizations, and look for online courses or podcasts about pet care and nutrition.

Pet Sitters International (PSI)

Pet Sitters International (PSI) is a professional association for pet-sitters. You can join for $155, which then becomes $145 annually. PSI offers a number of tools and resources that can help you improve your business and learn more about the industry.

They have a comprehensive website that includes some great information and links to other useful sites. The association offers information on medical benefits, using employees and subcontractors, and other things you will want to know. The site, at www.petsit.com, is also helpful for those just in the thinking stages.

PSI offers a certification program for members, which allows you to become an accredited pet-sitter for less than $300. When you complete the program, you receive certificates to display, pins to wear, and other items that signify your education as a pet-sitter.

PSI also offers liability insurance and bonding for members, credit card processing services, as well as an annual conference and regional meetings. To contact PSI, visit the website; email info@petsit.com; write to Pet Sitters International, P.O. Box 457, Pfafftown, NC 27040; or call (336) 983-9222.

Rounding Out Your Resume

You certainly want to flaunt any professional experience you had in pet-related jobs. If you worked for a veterinarian, don't just hide that fact on page two of your resume—include it in your marketing materials! You don't have to include the name of the veterinary practice on your marketing materials, but you should include it on your resume. Working with a veterinary practice is great not only for gaining some expertise but also for getting referrals for your pet-sitting services. Pet owners are quick to ask their veterinarian for that kind of information. Most veterinary practices won't "endorse" specific businesses, but many keep a notebook or bulletin board of local pet-related services that clients might be interested in.

Contracts, Insurance, and Legal Matters

Running a business is great when it runs smoothly but can bring headaches when you have legal entanglements or other mishaps. The best way for an entrepreneur to sleep comfortably at night is by having protections in place. This often starts with a very basic contract that you will put together with the help of a lawyer, one who specializes in contracts.

Contracts

Many people are uncomfortable with contracts. If you feel it is too much to ask customers to sign legal contracts for services, it's time to get over it. A written contract for your services makes it clear exactly what services you will provide, hence it can be defined as a service contract. Your contract should include when you will provide the services (or at least how many total hours a week if the specific times need to be flexible), what is expected of your client, when payment is expected, and what happens if payment is not made in a timely manner.

The contract should also include an outline of your fee structure, a limited liability statement, and a description of how services will be rendered. You can also include a warranty.

Don't simply buy a pad of legal contracts at the local office supply store—your business is unique, and you will want your contract to reflect that. It is almost imperative that you hire an attorney to draft your contract or to at least look over a draft contract you draw up. While attorneys fees can add up fast, they are well worth it for a customized service contract that you will use over and over. And as your business matures and expands, you can have your attorney tweak your contract to include any changes to your business.

In Chapter 8, you will find a sample service contract on page 100-102 used by an existing pet-sitting business, as well as a couple of other forms that will help clarify the arrangement between you and each of your customers. Look over these samples to help prompt your thinking about what you need in your contract.

Potential legal issues should be addressed in your contract. The contract should include the following points:

► What should happen in the event the pet gets seriously ill and needs veterinary care? Who decides what to let the veterinarian do? What is the owner's attitude about extreme measures?

► What should happen in the event the pet dies under your care?

► The owner should confirm by their signature that the pet has not been cited for having bitten someone in the past. Unless you have specific expertise with aggressive animals, you might want to stay away from clients whose pets have bitten. It's unfortunate and most of the time the pet was provoked, but it is ultimately a fact that pets who have bitten once are considered dangerous and likely to bite again. You need to decide how much risk you are willing to take.

Again, don't wait for these situations to happen before you address them. In the emotional and sometimes heated aftermath of an event like a dog bite, you will wish you had thought this through ahead of time.

Insurance

Because pet-sitting is just about caring for cuddly animals, you don't need to worry about insurance and other legal protections, right? Wrong! You always need to be sure you protect your own assets, such as your savings, your house, and your car. It just makes sense.

A pet-sitting business involves all the legal issues that are pertinent to any small business as well as some issues that are unique to pet care.

There are several types of insurance you should consider and a few you want to make sure you have. Some, like health, are personal insurance, but others are business oriented, like liability insurance, bonding, and workers' compensation.

Liability Insurance

You definitely need to be sure you are fully insured with liability insurance that covers you in the event that, say, a pet dies while under your care, and the owner decides you are responsible for the pet's death and sues you. But other potential instances of liability can occur that you may not think of until they happen.

For instance, what would happen if a client's dog bit a child while you were exercising the animal in the park? The dog may have been to the park every day for the past five years and played happily with all the children, but it only takes one day, one child, and one bite for a potentially nasty lawsuit.

A rider on your homeowners policy is typically how small businesses with extremely low revenue and a modest amount of foot traffic to the home cover their liability insurance needs. However, for a pet-sitting business where most of your business is done off-site, you need a separate liability policy.

Bonding

Nicknamed "honesty" insurance, bonding is this mysterious little insurance policy that you need to get for any business where you are entrusted with valuables, like the key to someone's

tip

Don't assume that just because you have insurance you don't need to worry about things that could lead to lawsuits. You should regularly review and update your contracts and other legal agreements. Have set policies about how you handle people's pets. Keep your automobile safe and maintained, and never transport a client's pet unless it is confined in a crate or safely harness. Insurance companies will expect you to take appropriate measures to avoid lawsuits to begin with.

tip

Amy C. of Maine recommends that all pet-sitters, especially those who take clients' dogs for walks, learn how to break up a dog fight. Specific techniques are described in Chapter 8. Liability surrounding injury to other animals and the pet you are sitting for is addressed in the sample contract in Chapter 8.

home and all the contents in it. Bonding ensures the client that you are trustworthy, and if they prove otherwise, the insurer provides them compensation.

Disability Insurance

Being self-employed, you should attempt to obtain disability insurance that covers you if you can no longer do the job you are trained for. For instance, if an injury renders you unable to drive for an extended period of time, you will want disability insurance that at least covers you until you can either retrain yourself for a different occupation, redirect your business, sell your business, or resume your business at the level it was before you were injured. Disability insurance can be very costly and difficult to get. If you do get it at a manageable rate, don't ever give it up!

Health Insurance

Many self-employed people scrimp when it comes to health insurance. Yes, it can take a big chunk of money each month to pay the premium. But it takes just one major illness to put you under financially.

First, depending on the illness, you may not be able to work at all or at the level you normally do. This instantly means a reduction in your income.

And second, consider the medical bills. Not only are you facing reduced income because you can't work, but you also must pay all your medical expenses.

If you really calculate it, paying, say, a $350-a-month premium for insurance that has a low ($15 to $30) co-pay and covers things like chiropractors, physical therapists, eye care, and other add-ons will ultimately pay you back if you take care of yourself and use these medical

tip

Be wary of taking on pets as clients with what is in the legal world called *known propensities*. In other words, if a dog has been in the court system because the dog bites, you will be putting your business (and yourself, and perhaps your employees or others) at risk. Of course, most dogs bite because of very specific circumstances. But in the courts, it doesn't really matter why the dog bit if it has had a confirmed reputation for biting before—you can easily risk your insurance company not covering you because you took an undue risk.

professionals. Regular physicals, blood work, and a couple of visits a year to a chiropractor can all add up pretty fast.

Do consider dental insurance as well. It's actually not too expensive—with premiums of around $50 a month. If you add up the costs for two cleanings, checkups, and annual X-rays, you might pay more for these services than you would in annual premiums ($600). And if you need more significant dental work, you will potentially be beyond the two-year window that, in some cases, you must have the insurance for before you can do certain major dental procedures.

Auto Insurance

Be sure to check your existing auto policy to see if it covers any accidents that might happen while you are using your car for business purposes. With some agencies, you are required to get a rider on your policy. Some agencies won't cover you at all. A more likely scenario is that you need to take out a commercial policy on your vehicle.

Liberty Mutual Insurance Company, for example, requires a commercial policy if the automobile is registered in the business's name. If the car is registered in your personal name, you need to insure it under a "business classification" only if the vehicle contains business signage. If you only travel locally, you might not want to pay for business insurance as long as you are not transporting the animals. Be sure to check with your auto policy for any special circumstances for transporting other people's pets (Liberty Mutual, for instance, requires no additional riders on the basic auto policy). What would happen if you had an accident while a client's pet was in your car? Pets are usually legally considered to be "property" of their owners. If the pet were, heaven forbid, to die in the accident, the owner would be compensated for the pet's monetary value, which is typically only the amount the animal is actually worth as a pedigreed (or not) animal.

Of course, we hope none of these things will ever happen, but by being protected, you don't have to learn the consequences after the fact.

tip ⓘ

Find an insurance broker who will look for the best insurance policies for you. Some brokers deal in only one or two types of insurance, but they have access to additional information at their fingertips. Your insurance broker will also come to know your priorities—for instance, whether you want the best health insurance for a reasonable cost or whether you simply want it as cheaply as you can get it. At renewal time, your broker will send you a menu of options and recommendations based on their knowledge of the current status of the insurance market and what you need or want out of a policy.

Legal Issues

Covering yourself legally is important in any business. Don't let the pet part of your pet-sitting business lull you into thinking you are just feeding the cute little poodle. What legal issues could occur? Let me assure you, there are lots.

You take the risk on yourself if you get bitten by a client's pet. This means you should be careful about the clients you take on. Add a line to your client contract that is similar to the one used by veterinarians when vaccinating your pet against rabies: "I, the undersigned, swear that to the best of my knowledge [name of pet] has never bitten anyone." And you should take all precautions and learn as much as you can about handling whatever animals you agree to care for. Having certificates of completion from a respected dog obedience school or animal training school won't stop you from getting sued, but this training would help demonstrate to a jury that you take your responsibilities seriously, you know how to handle dogs, and this particular situation was a fluke and not the result of inadequate knowledge or negligence on your part.

Besides liability issues, legal aspects to every business exist that you need to take seriously.

Corporate Structure

The first major legal decision you will make about your pet-sitting business should be deciding how your business will be structured. As discussed in Chapter 2, your main choices are among the following:

▶ Sole proprietorship
▶ Partnership
▶ Limited partnership
▶ Corporation

The choice you make will have a huge effect on how any legal issues are handled and resolved. The choice of sole proprietorship is the simplest, but it also means all your personal belongings are at risk. Incorporating is the most complex, and it is also more expensive and more complicated when it comes to legal issues.

Employees

If you want to keep your business simple, avoid hiring employees. Employees complicate a business, from legal requirements to taxes to personality conflicts. But if you want to grow your revenue and expand your services, employees will probably be a necessity.

Other ways to get help also exist when your business is expanding beyond your ability to keep up. Subcontractors (who work for themselves, not you, also called independent contractors) can be a great interim (or permanent) step when taking on more clients. But in any service business, you need to pick your subcontractors very, very carefully. They are, after all, representing you and the hard work you have done to create a certain level of care as well as a business flair and personality.

When hiring either employees or subcontractors, review their resumes to see if they have worked in service positions in which they had to deal directly with clients. This is a client-based business, meaning dealing with the pet owners. You need to look for people who know how to be attentive to the clients' needs. You also need people who are familiar with, and comfortable with, animals. Besides having their own pets, have they taken care of a neighbor's pets at any time? Do they have pet allergies?

Ask how they would respond to certain situations. Make sure they have a schedule that allows them availability during the times you most need help. Most important, try to determine how responsible they are—this is important to the success of your business. If they say they will be there at 3:00, they must arrive at 3:00 or slightly earlier. They also need to have reliable transportation. Always ask for business references, and then call a few of them.

Independent Contractors

You will probably get most of your outside help by using independent contractors or subcontractors. This situation may be able to carry you through all your needs without ever hiring actual employees. Although subcontractors carry their own insurance, you also need to be sure to add them to your insurance policy as well.

Noncompete and Confidentiality Agreements

If you hire a subcontractor, that person probably also contracts their services out to other pet-sitters, either in your market area or outside it. You don't want your subcontractor telling other employers any details they learn about your business while filling in or taking overflow work for you. A confidentiality agreement covers this and other situations, such as not sharing copies of contracts and other forms you have created (or paid someone else to create) for your business.

Noncompete agreements simply state that an employee cannot start their own pet-sitting business in your market area and usurp your clients. If you do not have employees, this is a nonissue. Subcontractors do not work for you, so it is difficult to institute much in the way of legal agreements. That said, you certainly should include a line in your subcontractor agreement that states that your client list is the property of your business.

Nothing can actually prevent employees or subcontractors from soliciting your clients to draw them to another business. However, a signed agreement is a legal document in which employees or subcontractors explicitly agree not to do this; if they do, you then have to decide whether it is worth pursuing legal action.

All that being said, most of your subcontractors will be people looking for part-time work while going to school or doing other jobs. Few people, in general, are entrepreneurial, and those that are may simply learn from you and eventually go off on their own. If your business is good and your customers like working with you, it is unlikely someone else will steal your customers.

Workers' Compensation

If you have an employee, you must carry workers' compensation insurance, which covers employees if they get injured while performing their job responsibilities. The purpose is to avoid lawsuits resulting from on-the-job injuries. Workers' compensation is administered under both federal and state statutes. To find out more, check out the workers' compensation information from the Department of Labor at www.dol.gov.

Internal Revenue Service (IRS) Obligations

As an employer, you are obligated to withhold a certain amount for income taxes, usually a percentage based on the information the employee provides on a W-4 form filled out at hiring. You also must withhold Social Security/Medicare taxes (that famous FICA line on the W-2). Not only do you withhold the employee's share, but you, the employer, also contribute an equal amount totaling, at the time of this writing, 15.3 percent of the employee's total salary, meaning you withhold 7.65 percent of their pay while also contributing 7.65 percent.

But wait, there's more. With employees, Uncle Sam also dips into your profits by requiring that you pay unemployment taxes. Check the IRS website (www.irs.gov) for the current amount you need to withhold. Your accountant can help you keep track of all these requirements.

Lastly, you may need to make these payments monthly, depending on the total. The IRS likes to make sure you keep up and don't get socked with a huge amount due all at once that you can't come up with.

If you hire employees, be sure to keep up with these employment-related tax payments. You can see how it pays to calculate just how much additional business an employee will bring in and if it is worth the additional expense (don't forget to calculate in the additional fees to your accountant and, potentially, your attorney).

Ultimately, if your business growth is pointing to the need for an employee, by all means start the hiring process. But don't take on the costs unless they are necessary. A growing business will prompt you to do one of two things:

▶ Add more people, add more services, implement new technology to keep tabs on your client data, and/or even expand your location.

▶ Stop expanding at the point where you are happy with the size of your business (financially and personally), and either create a waiting list for your services or contact other pet-sitters and tell them you have reached the maximum amount of

▶ Finding an Attorney

Don't wait until you need an attorney to find one. If you own a business, you will need an attorney at some point for something. Here are some ways to find the best attorney for you:

▶ Ask friends and family for referrals.

▶ Call and chat with the attorney or the office receptionist. Get a sense of how the firm conducts business and what kind of reception you might get if you call.

▶ Make sure you pick someone who has small-business experience and is more likely sensitive to the legal needs of a small-business owner.

▶ You probably won't find someone with experience specifically in pet-sitting, but look for an attorney who has experience in small service-industry businesses.

▶ Find out upfront what the attorney's rates are, what the standard fees are, how payment is expected, whether you can pay with credit cards, etc. Don't let the money part of it, which can be substantial, surprise you.

▶ Last, but far from least, be sure you feel comfortable and confident with the attorney's personality. You don't want to avoid consulting your attorney just because you don't like to talk with them.

Keep in mind that you are best served having an attorney available to review a few contracts upfront and when a need arises rather than having someone on a retainer whom you rarely ever need. Most small businesses have a relationship with an attorney that they call and pay as needed. Hopefully, this will be infrequently.

business you can handle. There's nothing wrong with maintaining a lucrative small business that provides you with a good lifestyle.

Having contracts, the best corporate structure for your business needs, and an attorney on your contact list are three ways to help secure your business and avoid the pitfalls and adversity that slow down the growth and success of a business. In the next chapter we'll discuss money issues, from bookkeeping to paying your taxes to getting help from an accountant.

Financial Considerations

I f financial matters are not your favorite topic, that view-

point must change when you decide to start your own

business. Finances probably won't ever reach as high on

your favorites list as taking care of animals, but all business

owners need to become intimately involved with the finances

of their businesses. You can choose to have someone else

take care of the nitty-gritty details, but you still want to understand the basics of your business's financial setup and what it all means to the success of your business. Without a financial core, a business is not a business; it is volunteer work. And if someone else is handling your financials, oversee what they are doing on a regular basis. It's your money, so make sure nobody is making costly mistakes or taking any home with them.

If you don't care about your business finances, you won't be in business long. You need to have the resources to maintain your vehicle and to simply buy gas—or the good credit to put gas on a credit card—to get to your jobs in the first place.

You have to decide some things about the finances of your pet-sitting business before you actually start up. You should have your books set up and be ready to record expenditures and revenue as soon as you begin putting out or taking in money for the business.

Class Act

Tanya K. of New Hampshire has an accounting degree and worked in the field for many years. And even she still has someone else do her books! But she admits it is critical to have a handle on the business finances end of things. "You at least need to be able to track your expenses," she says, as well as to understand why doing so is important.

One way to make the accounting and financial framework of your business less daunting is to take an accounting class. You can find many online classes, as well as articles, on basic accounting and/or managing finances for a small business. You can also check with your local Small Business Development Center (SBDC), which may offer small-business accounting classes or keep a list of classes offered through local community colleges or continuing-education programs at a local university.

Be logical when you sign up for an accounting class—don't sign up for a class that covers information beyond your current need or ability to understand. You don't need to know how to read the financial report of a $60 million international company to run your $20,000 local pet-sitting operation.

Cycles of the Financial Moon

First, you need to decide on your fiscal year. Sole proprietors should choose the calendar year as their fiscal year. Business income for a sole proprietorship will be reported on Schedule C on your personal tax return, which is filed according to the calendar year. (Don't worry, more on the dreaded "T" word later.)

Corporations operate under a different tax structure and can choose a fiscal year according to the logic of their business/industry. The pet-sitting business has two main busy periods of the year: vacation time and the holidays. Although people take vacations almost all times of year, the summer vacation time is the busiest because kids are out of school, followed closely by the time period between Thanksgiving and New Year's.

Keeping the Books

Unless you are setting up a pet-sitting empire right out of the box, you should be able to do your own day-to-day bookkeeping. If you have ever had even the smallest business or if you have ever worked for anyone else, you probably have heard this before, but it bears repeating: Keep every receipt for any dime you spend on the business. You don't have to carry your ledger around with you, but gather those receipts in one place and record them in your ledger at least weekly.

Set aside time for bookkeeping. These records tell you a lot about your business. You may notice patterns, expenditures that seem excessive, or other changes you could make for your business to be more efficient.

The Checkbook

Your checkbook will probably be the financial tool you use the most in the beginning. Because pet-sitting businesses often don't take a lot of capital to set up (unless you set up a boarding kennel, which we will discuss in Chapter 12 on expanding your business), you have to be careful not to fall into the trap of starting your business and simply using your personal checking account to pay for expenses and to deposit income.

Set up a separate checking account and designate it for the business. Pay for everything with this account, even if you use its debit card instead of actually writing a check. It doesn't have to be a "business" checking account—another personal account will do—just give the business an account all its own.

Not only is it good for keeping accurate track of expenses, but some psychological aspects result from having separate accounts and ledgers for taking yourself and your business seriously. Have the business name printed on your business-specific checking account—it lends an air of professionalism.

The Old-Fashioned Way

If you like a pen-and-paper approach to accounting, you can keep your books using an old-fashioned ledger notebook that you can still purchase in any office supply store or stationery store. Set it up for expenses and for income. At the end of each month, each quarter, or whenever you have designated, you can hand these ledgers over to your accountant, who will review them, balance them, let you know how much you still have for capital in your checking account, and perhaps even make suggestions of how to better keep your records. Your ledger, if well-kept, can tell you a lot about the day-to-day status of your business.

Software

Many software programs exist for easy setup of bookkeeping for your small business. Two commonly used ones are QuickBooks and Microsoft Office. Others with less well-known names are available as well, such as Big E-Z Bookkeeping. Whatever you use, make sure it's easy for small-business bookkeeping.

The main thing you need to keep in mind is that while these programs do many calculations and other useful things at the touch of a few keys on the keyboard, you still are required to set up the software in the first place and input the basic information, both initially and on an ongoing basis.

So if you think computerizing your books and doing it yourself is the easy way out, think again. No matter which method you decide on, you will need to put down the tug toy and spend time on the bookkeeping end of things. Set aside a large chunk of time to start, and then set aside time on an ongoing basis, maybe an hour weekly and a morning monthly.

Be sure to keep these software products up-to-date by logging in to the manufacturer's website periodically, or by signing up for automatic updates or reminders so you can keep as up-to-date as possible. Although the bookkeeping programs probably won't have as much in the way of updates, tax programs have constant updates.

If you know yourself well enough to know you are not going to set aside this time to feed your bookkeeping software, then hire an accountant. An upcoming meeting with your accountant encourages you to pull the information together, and you have a person who will nudge you to keep the appropriate records and provide the information needed to keep your finances accurate and up-to-date. Yet even with professional assistance helping you organize your books, it's to your advantage to understand various accounting methods.

Accounting Methods

There are two basic accounting methods: accrual and cash accounting. The accrual method of accounting is used in businesses where inventory is a factor. If you take on a line of products to sell, you may think about using accrual accounting. However, even if you do, you might want to set up the product line as a separate business from your pet-sitting business and use accrual accounting only for that business.

Cash accounting simply means you record an invoice as revenue when you send it out and you record an expense when you receive a bill that your business is supposed to pay. It is a very simple means of accounting.

No matter what method you use, you will need to create several kinds of financial statements, which we will describe next.

Making a Statement

Business owners use several statements to get an overview of their business and their financial status. These are:

▶ *Profit and loss statement (P&L).* This statement allows you to get a monthly picture of where your business stands that month, for the year-to-date, and compared to this time last year (either for the month or year-to-date).

▶ *Cash-flow statement.* This handy little statement lets you know how much money is coming into your business compared to how much went out.

▶ *Balance sheet.* The balance sheet balances all your business's assets against all its liabilities. How much you own is compared to how much you owe. This crucial statement lets you know how your business is faring financially at any moment in time, giving you the ability to make changes to shift the balance more in your favor. You can do some things to accomplish this, including:

- Increase the fee for your services.
- Get a more economical vehicle.
- Reduce the range of your market (if you are spending too much time or money to get to your jobs).
- Increase the range of your market (if you aren't getting enough jobs/customers).
- Stop billing customers and require payment at time of service.
- Find new suppliers of materials you need to keep on hand.

By the way, if you have a business plan, you may have included these numbers, but now they are known as *pro forma* statements because they are based on actual numbers.

Accountants

Bookkeeping and tax software may be enough while your business is still small with just a few clients. But as it grows, you should consider hiring an accountant to help with reviewing your numbers and filing taxes. While an accountant is an additional expense, it is a worthy investment. You don't have to use the accountant on a daily basis. Quarterly, at most, is probably enough to begin with. You can always increase your accountant's input to monthly when you have reached a certain level of revenue.

The important thing is that an accountant keeps you on track with your financial framework. Tax time is easier. Growth is easier. Getting additional capital to expand is easier. You can be ready to jump on unexpected opportunities, instead of having to re-create your financial history first because you didn't keep very complete records and aren't able to analyze or present your business from a financial perspective.

Set up an introductory meeting with at least a couple of accountants. You want to pick someone with whom you are compatible. You can weed out a couple of possibilities over the phone. One key question to ask your potential accountants is what kind of small-business experience they have in general and whether they have any experience with service-based businesses and pet-sitting businesses in particular. Then meet your finalists in person. A small fee may apply for this meeting, but it is well worth it to go with confidence into what you hope will be a long-term relationship.

Your best bet is getting a referral to a good accountant from someone you know and trust who also runs a small business.

Taxes

You can't get around it—being a business owner complicates tax time. This is another instance where having an accountant comes in handy. You need, however, to be sure your accountant is a tax accountant and not solely a bookkeeper. So many rules and layers apply to tax laws that having a tax-savvy accountant pays for itself in sheer savings on aspirin alone.

In an attempt to become more customer-friendly, the IRS has a fantastic website (www.irs.gov) that falls into the category of "more than you ever need or want to know." But if a topic involves federal taxes, it is there. You can download publications and forms to read on-screen or print out, which can save you on the evening of April 15th if you are scrambling to meet the deadline to complete your personal taxes.

One IRS publication that all small-business entrepreneurs should download or get a copy of is the *Tax Guide for Small Business* (Publication 334). Review it carefully and do your taxes in advance of April 15th so you can have your accountant review your work.

Keep in mind that any commonly accepted expenses in your business, such as leashes, collars, or specific cleaning supplies, or necessary expenses to keep your business running, such as your computer and perhaps client management software, can be listed as business expense deductions. Keep track of your expenses and save all documentation, such as receipts for anything you purchase, for the IRS.

Auto Expenses

Because traveling to your clients makes up a large chunk of your expenses for a pet-sitting business, you need to keep very detailed records of your automobile use. Keep a mileage log in your car, and get in the habit of using it every single time you slide behind the wheel, or get an app like Stride (www.stridehealth.com/tax), among others, that can help you keep track of your miles to and from clients and when picking up necessary business supplies.

You can record actual expenses for your vehicle—oil changes, tires, gas, etc. However, if you use the same vehicle for both personal and business use, it may be more expedient to simply use the IRS mileage rate (which, for the 2020 tax year, was 57.5 cents per mile, but check this every year because it changes almost annually). Otherwise, you need to carefully differentiate between uses, determine the percentage of use the car gets for business, and use that percentage when calculating taxable expenses for new tires, etc.

The key point here is that with this kind of business, automobile use can be a significant expense, and you should be sure to record every possible cent. This is not only important for tax purposes, but this is one of those places where hidden costs can eat away at your profits and you can't pinpoint exactly to where the money is disappearing. If you are commuting by bus or train, keep a list of your expenses and/or receipts of your expenditures, including tickets.

Client Invoices and Receipts

Even if you require payment on the spot, you always want to provide your client with an invoice for your services. This allows both of you to keep a record of your visits. Conscientious pet owners who are hiring pet-sitters most likely keep a notebook of information about their pets' care and health and will put these invoices in that notebook, so your work will be useful on all sides.

You want to establish some method of invoicing and giving receipts to clients. Depending on how fast your business plan shows your business increasing revenue and adding clients, you may want to think early on about having client software that keeps records of your clients. If you look to have only ten clients for the first year, you could create a spreadsheet using Excel (which is part of Microsoft Office). You probably don't want to spend the considerable money it would cost to install a business software package. But you should consider it as your business grows. A small-business client-based software package usually includes the capability of invoicing. You assign numbers to each of your services and, as the program asks you what to invoice for the client, you select the appropriate numbers for the services you provided and they automatically are listed on the invoice with an explanation and a price.

The other advantage to setting up this kind of program is the accumulation of client history. When clients call to book reservations for your services for their pets, you can look at the client's computer file and easily access all services you provided during previous visits. This allows you to personalize the call—"Does Fido still take phenobarbital twice a day?"—which gives a strong impression of reliability and a good feeling about how well you pay attention to that customer's pet.

You also can potentially add on services by saying things such as: "Last time we discussed having me walk Fido twice a day to help him be less anxious while you are gone. Would you like me to try that this time?" And you tack on an extra fee for an extra half hour of your time, or a fee per walk, or however you choose to set up your fee schedule.

tip

Do not fall into the trap of never paying yourself out of your business earnings. While it is important for a startup business to dump a lot of its revenue back into the business, burnout is one of the top reasons businesses fail. So if you work 60 hours a week, you should at least take enough money out of the business checkbook to treat yourself to a spa visit or whatever you find will recharge your batteries for the next 60-hour workweek!

The point is good record keeping not only helps you organize your business from a financial standpoint, but it also gives you opportunities to excel at customer service and client relationship-building by taking good notes about each pet client and their owners.

Payment Options

Do you want to allow your clients to use credit cards and debit cards? An added expense applies for this, but it can be very convenient for your client. The advantage to you is that with a credit card, you get payment on the spot, or with a debit card, you find out on the spot if the client's account doesn't have enough money—the card simply won't go through. A number of apps are available that let you accept payments.

The easiest manner in which to collect money in a business such as pet-sitting might be good old cash or a simple account transfer via an app like Venmo or PayPal because your fees are typically for only a few hours at a time. If you get to know and trust a client, you can switch to a weekly check if they prefer. If a check bounces, let the client know immediately, have them pay your part of the bank fee, and go back to cash for the time being.

A combination of payment options often works best. As your company grows, you'll want to look into having credit card options, such as the easy-to-use Square payment system, which allows you to use your cell phone as a mobile cash register (https://squareup. com). This will entail setting up a credit card merchant account, a bank account, and a way to process payments. Some startup payment fees and fees per transactions (which are usually around 2 to 4 percent) apply. The merchant account will allow you to accept payments through Visa, Mastercard, American Express, and other credit card companies. You can Google merchant services and compare options.

Policies

Every business that deals with customers (which is every business, small or large) needs to establish financial policies, and they need to be adhered to rigorously. If your policy is to require payment at the time of service, you need to stick to that policy for every customer, every time. Of course, you will always encounter an exception to the policy, but if every instance is an exception, then no longer are there exceptions because there aren't any rules!

Policies often are focused on payment- and money-related issues, but you may find you need to have policies for other areas, too. How many times will you visit any one client in a day? How many pets will you care for in one household? Perhaps you have a policy that you will not take a job caring for any dog who has ever bitten someone or had a complaint filed against him. The customers in this kind of business are unique; you will come up with your own issues to have policies for. But stick to your policies, or don't make them in the first place!

Collections

Speaking of policies, have a collections policy and absolutely stick with it. Don't let invoices add up. Rates are low enough that people should have cash or a check available every time. If you find you are embarrassed or shy about asking for overdue payment, you need to get over it immediately. You provided your part of the bargain; your customers need to pull through with theirs. As a business owner, you should always include net terms on invoices, so that at a minimum, you can hold your customers to those net terms. Also date your invoices and save a hard copy along with the one on your computer.

If a customer takes too long to pay, don't take on a new job for that client without at least a partial deposit. For those who take too long to pay more than once, you should require complete, upfront payment or simply not take on the job at all.

Paying Yourself

One of the perks of opening a low-cost, no-overhead business is you can usually start taking some money for yourself early on, while putting the rest into the business. If you know your ongoing expenses, you can cover them and have some money left over. If, however, you are looking to build a large pet-sitting business with offices and many employees, then—like most startups—you will need to put nearly all the money earned back into the business for the first year or two. This means you need to have some money set aside to help you pay your bills when starting the business. If you can afford to do this, that's great—you should probably plan to do this for at least the first year, depending on how complex a business you establish.

But there comes a point when you want to give yourself at least some pay. If you are independently wealthy, then pay yourself enough for some mad money. If your spouse has a fantastic job that provides for all the family's needs, great—pay yourself enough to do some home renovations, buy new furniture, or go on a couple of vacations a year.

Service businesses aren't like other businesses in which you build something that can be sold, and that is where you eventually make money. You certainly can sell your business—to someone wishing to start a pet-sitting business. It's much easier to buy a business that has an established customer base. However, if there isn't an entrepreneur hoping to buy an existing service business when you wish to sell, there really isn't much opportunity to sell to an existing pet-sitting business—existing business owners can just as easily wait for you to close your business and then be sure to have ads and fliers in places that will get in front of your customers' eyes. In other words, your competitors won't have to spend the money on buying your business; they can gain your customers' business much more cheaply.

So pay yourself something—there is some reward to feeling like your business is providing a financial return, even if it is just dinner out twice a week!

If you need to get a paycheck out of the business, you have to decide how much your paycheck should be and then figure out how many jobs you need to take in a given period to pay yourself that amount—minus expenses and some padding for the business, of course.

Raining Cats and Dogs

As a pet-sitter, the majority of your business is almost always predominantly caring for dogs and cats. Sitting for a dog and/or cat sometimes also entails caring for the family gerbil, guinea pig, parakeet, ferret, or rabbit. These are typically easy to manage. You can find out more about sitting for those animals in Chapter 9.

However, some pet-sitters focus on barn animals, which we will cover in Chapter 10.

Then in Chapter 11, we'll provide an overview of more exotic animals that may crop up here and there, keeping your pet-sitting experiences even more interesting than you might have imagined.

In this chapter, we'll cover the basic care for a variety of animals, starting with a review of some of what we have discussed previously for dogs and cats. We'll also expand the discussion with additional information on areas such as vaccinations, vital signs, and even infectious diseases humans can contract from pets.

Basic Dog Care

We are starting with dogs even though cats outnumber dogs as pets because, except for extended periods, most people with only cats as pets do not enlist the services of a pet-sitter. The cat can be easily fed by a responsible neighbor. Of course, the litter box situation also needs taking care of.

The basics of caring for a dog are the same for all sizes and breeds. The dog needs to be fed at regular intervals, have fresh water, get time outside to do his business, and get a bit of exercise and companionship.

Feeding

Always feed the dog (or any pet for that matter) exactly what the owner tells you to. During your initial visit you'll learn where the food is kept. Be sure the owner outlines the details, such as whether the dog typically gets water in his dry food, whether his canned food is mixed with the dry, or whether they are served separately. This information can save the animal some stress and can save you some stress as well; you may worry the dog is sick if he turns up his nose at his supper simply because it is not prepared in the usual way.

Here are some other questions to ask the owner about the dog's feeding time:

tip

Always be sure to keep a dog's food supply somewhere the dog cannot get to it. Even if the owner assures you the dog never gets into the food bag, animals act differently when their owners are away. The dog may get more bored than usual or may be stressed out by the fact their owner is away. A dog who has overeaten is a very sick dog and may require a trip to the veterinarian to have their stomach pumped. A dog can even die if they eat excessively and get too full and stomach twisting occurs.

Likewise, put bread, cookies, and other edibles high up or in the fridge, or store them in the microwave, out of temptation's way.

▶ Is the dog normally a fussy eater? If she is, you will know not to be alarmed if she doesn't wolf down her entire dinner in a flash.

▶ Is there a specific place the dog likes to eat? If his dinner is always served in the same place, be sure to set the bowl there, too. Pet-sitting is intended to help the dog be more comfortable when his owner is away, so you need to provide these little consistencies.

▶ If you are caring for more than one dog and they eat different foods, do they need to be locked away from each other during feeding? You don't want them eating each other's food and becoming sick, especially if one gets a prescription-type dog food and one doesn't.

One last thing: Even if the owner tells you the dog doesn't at all mind being approached while they are eating, don't bother them unless it's absolutely necessary. Dogs can be very possessive about their food, and it is just not worth the risk of being bitten.

Water

Water is vital. Do not scrimp on water because you're worried that too much might cause Fido to pee in the

tip

Unless a pet is being starved or otherwise shows obvious nutritional neglect, or you are specifically asked for advice, the food choices the owner makes for their pet are not your business; your business is to feed it to them. Most owners that are responsible enough to hire a pet-sitter are also bringing their pets for regular veterinary checkups (something you should require anyway to be sure the animals are vaccinated), so let the client's veterinarian take care of client education regarding food.

▶ Vaccination Requirements

People have different philosophies about vaccinations, but you should know the vaccine status of any pet you care for. Dogs should be up-to-date on the vaccine that covers distemper, hepatitis, leptospirosis, parvovirus, and parainfluenza. Also check state regulations on rabies vaccinations and require that your clients comply. If your pet-sitting job includes bringing Fido to day care, he will need to be vaccinated against kennel cough.

Cats should be up-to-date on vaccines for three diseases: panleukopenia, rhinotracheitis, and calicivirus. Cats should also follow a veterinarian-recommended rabies vaccination schedule, although many states do not as yet regulate rabies vaccinations in cats.

▶ Poison Control Center

The American Society for the Prevention of Cruelty to Animals (ASPCA) runs a poison control center. The emergency number is (888) 426-4435. A $65 consultation fee applies, for which you will need to provide a credit card. If the pet is enrolled in ASPCA Pet Health Insurance, you will receive 90 percent off this fee. The poison control center's staff can provide information on dogs, cats, and various other pets, as well as livestock. You can familiarize yourself with what the ASPCA offers at www.aspca.org/pet-care/animal-poison-control.

house. Cleaning up a little pee on the floor is a lot better than having a dog in your care get sick from dehydration or constipation. Find out how much he regularly drinks during the course of a day so you know what his normal water consumption is, and then leave double that amount each time you visit.

Treats

Find out what kind of treats the owner gives their dog, where the treats are kept, and how many the dog usually gets per day. Give the dog only those kinds of treats, unless you ask otherwise. Some pet owners are happy to have their dogs receive any kind of special treats; others are picky about what their pets eat. No matter your feelings about what a dog should get for food or treats, this is not your dog.

Toys

Leave out only toys that are allowed by the owners. Some toys that are billed as indestructible last only five minutes in the mouth of a vigorous dog. And only give toys meant for dogs—this includes flying discs. Frisbees and other plastic discs found in the children's toy department can be very hard on dogs' teeth and gums. Lighter-weight discs are made especially for dogs.

Dog Restraint

Before we get into some basic first aid, you should know how to restrain a dog so you can perform simple procedures, such as taking their temperature or transporting an injured animal. Collars, harnesses, and muzzles are all useful forms of restraint when dealing with dogs. Find out the preference of the owner before using anything.

Keep in mind that injured dogs may react violently even to their owners, even if the animal is normally very friendly. The dog may be in pain or disoriented. Be sure to muzzle an injured dog—keep a couple of different-size muzzles in your vehicle.

You can fashion a makeshift muzzle out of anything that has some length to it and is soft—a necktie or a rag, for example. Fold the item in half to make a loop and quickly get it around the dog's nose. Cross it under the chin and tie the ends behind the ears. Be sure the cloth is snug enough not to come loose but not so snug at the throat as to injure the dog or cut off their air supply.

Vital Signs

You should know something about dog and cat first aid. The most important thing to know is how to determine the animal's vital statistics and what is considered normal. It's always nice if the owner has the animal's baseline vitals written down somewhere, but many owners don't know this information about their animals.

Temperature

The normal temperature range for a dog is between 100 and 102.5 degrees Fahrenheit, a little higher than humans. A dog's temperature is taken in the rectum. For cats, you can use a rectal thermometer or a digital ear thermometer. The normal body temperature for cats falls in the range of 99.5 to 102.5. Although veterinarians are still stuck on the old mercury thermometers, digital thermometers that you can buy in the drugstore are easy to use and easy to read. It's often a two-person job to take a dog or cat's temperature with one person holding the animal and the other holding the thermometer in place.

▶ Dog Fight Savvy

Amy C. of Maine says the most important thing you need to know if you take dogs for walks is how to break up a dog fight. "Very few people know the proper, safe techniques to do this," she says. If there are two people, each should grab one dog's hind legs. "The dog," says Amy, "may transfer its aggression to you, so move the dog in a circle to keep the front end occupied." Amy recommends always carrying pepper spray. "This may seem harsh," she says, "but it is mild compared to what can happen in a serious dog fight."

You will, of course, want to know that the dog is OK with having their temperature taken. Even if the animal is normally even tempered, they may be a bit testier if sick, so proceed with caution. Put petroleum jelly or another lubricant on the end of the thermometer, or use little sanitary sleeves (a few are often provided with the thermometer), lift the dog's tail, and insert the thermometer about an inch. The digital thermometer beeps when it has remained at the same temperature for a certain period of time, indicating the highest reading has been attained.

Pulse

The normal pulse rate depends on the size of the dog. Larger dogs have a slower pulse. Check the pulse by pressing in the groin area inside the hind leg up near the abdomen. This is the femoral artery. Once you have located the pulse, count for 15 seconds then multiply by four to get the beats per minute. The normal range for a large dog is 60–90 bpm; for a medium dog, 70–110 bpm; and for a small dog, 90–120 bpm.

tip

Pets should not be fed chocolate in any form. Chocolate contains a naturally occurring compound called theobromine, which causes a spike in adrenaline, leading to a racing heart and even coma, depending on the amount consumed.

Another no-no for pets is onions, which contain a substance that can lead to anemia.

▶ Pet Vital Signs

The following are average vital signs for dogs and cats. Remember, all of these can be influenced by external factors such as excitement level and ambient temperature.

	Pulse (beats/minute)	Temperature (degrees F)	Respiration (breaths/minute)
Large Dogs (100+ lbs.)	60–90	100–102.5°	15–30
Medium Dogs (50–100 lbs.)	70–110	100–102.5°	15–30
Small Dogs (under 50 lbs.)	90–120	100–102.5°	15–30+
Cats	150–200	99.5–102.5°	20–30

Respiration

Normal respiration for a dog is between 15 and 30 breaths per minute. You can test this by putting your hand to the dog's nose and counting the exhalations.

Capillary Refill Time

Another checkpoint in a potentially ill animal is how long it takes for blood to return to tissue, called capillary refill time (CRT). The best place to check this is the gums. Gently lift the dog's upper lip and press your finger hard enough on the gum to drain the spot of blood. Remove your finger and watch how long it takes for blood to refill the area. It should refill immediately and within a second or two look like the surrounding tissue. If it is slow or if the gums seem excessively pink, mention this when you call the veterinarian.

tip

If you have a pet-sitting business and are pregnant, you need to stay away from cat litter boxes. Cat feces can transfer the parasite that causes toxoplasmosis, which can harm the fetus if contracted by a pregnant woman. Find a subcontractor for jobs with cats or simply refuse jobs that entail cat care until you have delivered your baby and are back to work.

Basic Cat Care

Many of the same aspects that are important for caring for dogs are important for cats. Be sure you know exactly what the cat normally eats and where they are fed. If a dog also lives in the house, you probably need to be sure to keep the cat's food dish out of reach of the dog. The cat may typically drink out of the dog's water bowl, but it would be best to leave the cat her own water dish. Unlike dogs, who may run up to you and start licking you, cats are often more standoffish at first. Let them come to you when they are ready. Cats have very distinct personalities, and many will warm up to you slowly and become very affectionate, while others will want to keep their distance. Therefore, you may not want to stand there waiting for them to eat. Back away from the food or go into the other room, and check later to see if the cat did or did not eat. Unlike dogs, who are always ready to eat, cats will eat only when they are hungry. Some may wait until you leave to eat, so know how much food you've left in the bowl, and perhaps make an extra visit if the cat does not eat while you are there to see if the food is gone later.

Cat Restraint

Cats can be much less tractable than most dogs. Of course, exceptions always exist. And cats who you might assume would give you a lot of trouble sometimes stay rock still while being examined—presumably they think if they just cooperate, they won't be hurt!

One simple way to thoroughly restrain a cat is with a thick towel (a good reason to keep a thick towel in your vehicle supplies). Make sure all four legs and feet are thoroughly wrapped. Hold the animal snugly enough that they can't get away but not so snugly as to encourage them to want to struggle. Another method is "scruffing"— hold the cat pretty snugly by the scruff of the neck, hold the back legs and tail with the other hand, and stretch the cat out into a firm but gentle arch. A lot of how you choose to restrain a cat depends on what you need to do and how much the cat is accustomed to being handled.

▶ From Pet to You

Several infectious diseases are transferable from dogs, cats, and other animals to humans. These are called *zoonoses*. You should know what they are and their basic signs.

- ▶ *Cat Scratch Disease*. This disease is contracted through a skin-penetrating bite or scratch from a cat. It can cause flu-like symptoms in general and/or mild to severe swelling at the bite site. Recovery typically occurs without treatment, although antibiotics are sometimes required.

- ▶ *Orf*. Orf is a herpes-like virus that causes skin lesions. It is contracted from direct contact with infected goats and sheep, who show signs all around their mouth and nose areas. Orf typically goes away on its own and its symptoms are mild to severe. If you care for animals with orf (also called cold sores), use gloves and try not to handle the animals. Orf is very contagious.

- ▶ *Rabies*. This viral infection affects the central nervous system and is deadly. You should require that all dogs and cats you care for be vaccinated for rabies. And you should get vaccinated as well. If you are bitten or scratched by a dog or cat, there is a definite protocol. If the animal has an up-to-date vaccination record and has been recently vaccinated, then the situation should be fine. If the animal is not vaccinated, then it needs to be quarantined and perhaps euthanized, depending on state regulations.

- ▶ *Toxoplasmosis*. This parasite, as mentioned in the tip about pregnancy on page 101, is passed from cat feces (a good example of why it is important to wash your hands after handling animals, cleaning litter boxes, etc.) and can cause mononucleosis-like symptoms.

Although wearing thick gloves seems sensible, they are usually not very effective—ones that are thick enough to fend off a cat bite often are so awkward you can't do what you need to do. Again, ask the owners how they prefer you restrain their cat.

The key is to use the appropriate level of restraint you think you might need—too much might panic the animal, too little isn't effective enough.

Allergies

If you have cold symptoms that don't go away, you might have an allergy to cats or dogs. You can make a visit to an allergist for testing, which is typically a skin test. This is where they prick your skin with a tiny amount of something you may be allergic to, which is often dog or cat dander. Depending on the degree of your allergies, you can buy over-the-counter products or may need a prescription for something stronger from your doctor. Dogs may have allergies if you notice symptoms such as itchiness; hives; swelling of the face, ears, or eyelids; inflamed skin; diarrhea; sneezing; or itchy eyes. Cats may have similar symptoms, including sneezing, coughing (if the cat has asthma), wheezing, itchy skin/increased scratching, itchy runny eyes, itchy back or base of tail, itchy ears and ear infections, vomiting, diarrhea, snoring caused by an inflamed throat, swollen paws, or paw chewing. Food allergies in cats may be evident if they are frequently scratching at their heads and necks, as well as have gastrointestinal problems like diarrhea and vomiting. Dogs can also have food allergies. If these symptoms occur in the pets you are sitting for, let the owner know so they can take the pet to the veterinarian for allergy testing.

Basic First Aid

The two most important things you can do when it comes to first aid for pets under your care are to:

1. Have veterinarian numbers on hand, including the number of the pet's regular veterinarian and the closest off-hours emergency clinic.
2. Take a pet first aid class from the Red Cross or anywhere that gives one locally. Or at least spend some time with a veterinarian or vet tech to learn some of the basics.

Signs of Illness

The key signs of illness in most pets are lack of appetite, vomiting, diarrhea, or lethargy. If the pet normally greets you enthusiastically at the door, you should be suspicious if they don't. When you call the veterinarian, it is helpful to have taken the pet's vital signs, though someone at the veterinarian's office will retake them the minute the pet is in the exam room.

Look around for any evidence that the pet ate something—a loaf of bread or some other item off the counter; a wrapper or remnants of a plastic item; or anything else to indicate the animal (typically a dog) may have a foreign object in their stomach or is ill from overeating or eating something that shouldn't be ingested.

If the dog vomited or had diarrhea but is otherwise acting normally—attentive, interested in playing, eating normally—then you may be dealing with an isolated incident. If vital signs are normal, and the pet greeted you normally, was eager to go out, and was excited to eat their meal, then you can probably leave the dog for the day or night with confidence. If you are still concerned even though the dog is now acting normally, come a little early for the end-of-day visit in case you then feel a trip to the veterinarian might be in order (you can save your client an emergency call if the pet is seen while the regular clinic is still open). Or you may want to stop back for an extra visit to check on the pet. You will need to be sure your fee schedule lists what such an extra visit costs so the owner is prepared. Although you want to be sure to be compassionate and give the best care for the animal, you don't need to do that for free. And you should always call the owner first to discuss the pet's condition.

▶ First Aid Kit

The following items will run you $50 to $75 depending on how much you buy, what the quality is, and what type of container you choose to store them in. But you should have a kit that contains:

- ▶ A stethoscope
- ▶ A digital thermometer
- ▶ Lubricant
- ▶ Alcohol
- ▶ Cotton swabs
- ▶ Tape
- ▶ Latex gloves
- ▶ Scissors
- ▶ Tweezers
- ▶ Antibiotic ointment

Similar considerations should be taken for cats. The key is whether the animal is now acting normally even though it had an accident on the floor.

Wound Care

Another first aid situation you may come across is wound care—a cut from broken glass or any other number of problems dogs are capable of getting themselves into, especially if you let them out or they stay out for the day.

The first thing you want to do is stop or slow the bleeding and determine if the wound needs stitches. Dogs commonly cut their pads, and these cuts can be very deep; they often don't require stitches, but they need to be cleaned and wrapped.

Neither dogs nor cats are really happy about having bandages—there is almost no place on their bodies that you can put a bandage that they won't work at tearing it off.

Puncture wounds are the ones to watch out for. If the pet gets a puncture-type wound (as opposed to a slice-like cut), it is best to have the veterinarian check it out. Puncture wounds close up on the surface, leaving a breeding ground for all sorts of bacteria from the cause of the puncture. Puncture wounds demand careful cleaning that is best left to the veterinarian and may require prophylactic antibiotic injections.

Client Attitude

Spend a little time in the initial interview talking with your clients about their own attitudes about veterinary care for their pets. Be sure to fill out a service contract (Figure 8–1 on page 106). Chapter 2 contains a client profile worksheet (Figure 2–2 on page 27) for each new customer. Some people are more hands-on and take care of lots of things themselves—if they feel confident in your skills, they are probably fine with you caring for a relatively minor wound and will not expect you to run the pet to the veterinarian's office for every little thing. Other people bring their pet to the veterinarian for every little cut, scrape, runny nose, dirty ear, or hangnail.

You definitely don't want to be shy about getting the pet to a professional for something that concerns you—the pet is your responsibility, after all. Take a look back in Chapter 2 and be sure to complete a pet profile worksheet (Figure 2–3 on page 29) and an emergency notification (Figure 2–4 on page 31) on each new client. But as you become more and more familiar with your clients, and more experienced yourself, you will find these decisions become easier to make. Nonetheless, always call the pet owner and alert them to the situation.

Service Contract

This agreement is made the_____day of _____ between _____ (hereinafter "Handler") and_____(hereinafter "Owner").

1. *Purpose of Agreement.* The purpose of this agreement is to state the duties and obligations of the Handler and Owner, respectively, concerning the care and handling of the below described dog(s), horse(s), cat(s).

   Handler: _____

   Owner name: _____

   Address: _____

   Phone: _____

   Work phone: _____

   Cell phone: _____

   Email: _____

2. *Subject of Agreement.* The animals, which are the subject of this agreement, are fully described below. The Owner hereby affirms that the information provided is true and correct, and agrees to indemnify and hold harmless the Handler for any damages that may result to the animals, to the Handler, to the Owner, or to third parties from inaccurate information being provided herein:

   Information About the Animal(s)

   Breed: _____

   Color: _____

   Sex: _____

   Name: _____

   Date of birth: _____

   (Use separate pages for multiple animals)

FIGURE 8–1: **Service Contract**

Service Contract

The above described animals are referred to herein as "the Animals."

Health Information About the Animal(s)

Chronic illnesses: _____

Date of last rabies vaccine: _____

Name, address, and phone number of veterinarians: _____

_____

Behavior Information About the Animal(s)

Describe fully any previous displays of aggression of ANY TYPE (including aggression toward other animals or people): _____

_____

_____

3. *Authorization*. The Owner hereby authorizes and empowers the Handler to walk/exercise the Animals in the designated locations and public areas, enter the home, and feed the Animals.

4. *Indemnification and Hold Harmless*. The Owner hereby agrees to indemnify and hold harmless the Handler, or the Handler's duly authorized agent, from any and all liability that may result from the following: any injuries inflicted by the Animals on other animals, on the Handler, on the Owner, or on third parties; any injuries that may be suffered by the Animals; destructive behavior in the house/house soiling. (Valuables and sentimental items should be safely stored.)

5. *Emergencies*. In the event that emergency medical care is necessary for the Animals, it is agreed that the Handler will obtain such treatment from any licensed veterinarian, the expense of which will be reimbursed by the Owner within two business days.

    Emergency contact numbers: _____

    _____

FIGURE 8–1: **Service Contract,** continued

Service Contract

Relatives or other contact person (if the Owner cannot be reached): _____

_____

6. *Cleaning Procedure/Solutions*. The Owner must choose and leave the appropriate carpet cleaner for the Handler. Food dyes and natural pet body fluids can bleach and stain carpeting and are beyond the Handler's control.

7. *Keys.** The Owner must provide two sets of keys, one for the Handler to carry and one to leave at the Handler's home. Owner has checked that all keys work. Keys are not to be left hidden outside by the Owner or Handler.

Owner signature: _____ Date: _____

Print name: _____

Handler signature: _____ Date: _____

Print name: _____

Contact number where the Owner will be: _____

*Who else has a key to the Owner's house? _____

Courtesy Amy Carlson, Amy's Animal Care

FIGURE 8–1: **Service Contract,** continued

Other Common House Pets

You may encounter many pets other than dogs and cats in your pet-sitting adventures. Some of the more common ones are covered in this chapter. You typically are not hired to care for just these pets—unless a client has an entire aviary of finches. Most are animals you care for along with the family dog or cat.

The key to pet-sitting for any animal you are not familiar with is to be sure the owner tells you everything they know about caring for the animal on a daily basis. Of course, you don't need to know every detail about the breed or every aspect of medical care—you hope you won't need to deal with these things!

What you do need are clear instructions, preferably written, on the following:

tip

Be sure when you take on a type of animal that is new to you that the owner leaves you with a website, book, magazine, or other resource that they use themselves when they need to find out more information about something regarding their pet.

- ▶ *Feeding.* Be sure you know what kind of food the animal eats, how much, how often, what dishes are used, where the food is kept, and where it is bought.
- ▶ *Cleaning cages.* You need to know how often to clean the cage, what to use, what to use for bedding material, and what to do with the pet while you are cleaning the cage.
- ▶ *Exercise.* Are you expected to provide the pet with exercise time outside of what the pet gets in the cage? You need to know how long the sessions should be and how vigorous.
- ▶ *Signs of illness.* You cannot learn every detail about every animal's possible maladies, but do have the owner tell you about the ones that are most common and would be the most likely to show up if anything goes wrong while under your care.

No Free Lunch

If you take on a new client who has any (or, imagine, all!) of these other house pets in the mix, you need to set a fee schedule to add on to your basic dog- or cat-care fee. Don't get lured into thinking these little critters won't take up much extra time. That can be true, but it also can be true that some of them are a bit fussy to care for, and the risks of something happening to them are higher than for your typical cat or dog.

Adding at least a $5 fee per day or even per visit for each "extra" pet is legitimate and can help you avoid building any resentment that you need to fuss with these extra animals each time you visit.

Although any good pet-sitter takes the utmost care of any animal entrusted to them, you also need to remember that you are running a business. The extra ten minutes per visit that it takes to check on the cage of hamsters, fill food dishes and water, and even clean the cage is ten minutes that could be spent driving to your next job.

▶ All the Info

Now let's take a look at the *Merck Veterinary Manual*. This classic veterinary guide is a must-have for anyone who makes their living dealing with animals in any way. It has a wealth of information on a wide range of topics, compiled over 60 years and updated often.

Merck is a big name in both human and animal health and is a reliable source of fascinating information. The manual gets as technical as you would possibly want to get, but it also has lots of general information—such as overviews of categories of animals and introductory material about all kinds of animals—that any pet-sitter wanting to give high-quality care (which should be all of you!) would find intriguing. The manual can be ordered online as a reference book or found at some bookstores, if you can still find any bookstores. You can also access the *Merck Veterinary Manual* online for free at www.merckvetmanual.com. The site is highly searchable and includes thumbnails of all charts and figures, which you can click to see directly.

Saying No

You may not wish to care for some types of animals. You may even be allergic to some pets. Make sure it is perfectly clear in your marketing literature specifically what animals you will take on and which animals you will not; they can ask about others. If a client still wants you to care for their dogs and cats, perhaps a neighbor or relative can take home the cage of chameleons (or whatever people dream up to keep as pets). Some of these smaller animals are better kept somewhere someone is around most of the time anyway.

The key is to be clear with potential clients. Don't be wishy-washy and find yourself caring for animals you don't want to care for. On the other hand, if you are going into the pet-sitting biz, you may need to prepare yourself for anything.

While dogs and cats have been the two stars of the book thus far, we'll now cover specifics for other popular pets, including birds, rodents, fish, ferrets, rabbits, and reptiles.

Birds

Parakeets are the most common pet bird you will come across. Other birds include finches, cockatiels, and parrots of different varieties. You may run across more unusual birds as well, but unless you are pet-sitting at someone's medieval British castle, you probably won't happen upon too many peacocks to care for. Turkeys are not high in the pet statistics either, although chickens could be part of the mix if you are barn-sitting.

For short-term care, say a day or two, you probably don't need to do anything more than keep the water bottle filled and the feed trays cleaned and full of food. For this, you need to reach into the cage door. You need to know how to make sure the bird doesn't get out in the process. And for some of the larger birds in smaller cages, you need to be sure the bird won't bite you! You may ask the owner if they advise you wear gloves.

Chances are if the bird is kept as a pet, he won't bite, but animals can be funny with strange people. It is best to feed the bird once or twice while the owner is still around so the bird can get familiar with you while his owner is still there to help him feel comfortable.

When the bird's owner is away for more than a couple of days, you need to clean the cage as well as keep food and water dishes full. Have the pet owner show you how to do this. For instance, you should know what the owner typically does with the bird while cleaning his cage.

Some birds enjoy treats in addition to commercially prepared bird food. If the owner requests that you feed these treats, be sure the owner buys the food, stores it properly (e.g., refrigerated if necessary), and indicates exactly what food is intended for the bird. Sometimes one type of lettuce may be a special treat, and another kind may make the bird sick!

One of the most important things with birds is temperature control. If it is winter in a cold climate, you need to be diligent about checking that the furnace is running and the temperature is at the optimum level for the bird.

You probably need to cover the bird's cage at night with a towel or whatever the owner uses to cover the cage. The owner may also ask you to give the bird some flying time. This requires you follow specific instructions. The owner knows where the bird will fly and how to get the bird to come back to the cage. And make sure all windows and doors are closed. You'll be out of a job if the bird takes off and does not return. Birds of all kinds—finches, parakeets, parrots, mynah birds, cockatiels—can be fascinating to interact with. Once you get accustomed to caring for them, you may find them to be among your favorites.

Rodents

Hamsters and guinea pigs are common pets, especially in homes with children; rats and mice are also kept as pets. Again, they often don't require special care. However, their cages can get pretty smelly pretty fast. Cleaning rodents' cages is necessary if the pet owner is gone for more than a few days. Don't avoid this. It is not good customer service for your clients to come home refreshed from their vacation to find a filthy cage they must immediately clean.

Hamsters and guinea pigs sleep all day, and chew, run on the treadmill, or forage around all night. You may never see them in action during the times you are there. This makes it difficult to tell if they are OK, but you should be able to see whether they ate and drank during the course of the night. If your care spans a long enough period, say a week, then you will need to take the rodent out of the cage to clean it (the cage, not the rodent). The owner will tell you specifically where to put the rodent while cleaning the cage. Make sure it cannot get out but has some means of air. Never underestimate the small spaces rodents can get through.

The owner should leave plenty of food and treats for the animal. Some people like to give their pet rodents some fresh greens and keep a supply in the refrigerator. Remove uneaten fresh food each day because it can go bad.

Always freshen the pet's water at every visit. In fact, it wouldn't hurt to be sure to leave two tubes of water.

Fish

After hamsters and guinea pigs, fish are probably the most popular pets for kids. You will often run across fish in your jobs taking care of dogs and cats, although the fish probably are not the main reason you're hired.

Fish don't require a lot, but their care can be time consuming. You need to know how much to feed them and if you will have to clean the tank. The most important thing to find out is what to do if the pump and filter stop working.

You should know what the owner would like you to do if you find a fish floating upside down when you arrive at the home. You can do some things for a fish who seems under the weather—one sign of a sick fish is that it isolates itself from the group.

According to the Animal Network, the following things are critical when it comes to fish tanks:

- ► Excellent water quality
- ► A balanced diet
- ► Compatibility among fish in tank
- ► Low stress level

Overfeeding is a problem because the food that goes uneaten affects the quality of the water. Your care helps to maintain all these factors.

Water is best changed at 10 to 15 percent of the tank once a week. If you are providing long-term care for a client's aquarium, you should plan to provide a partial water change for the tank during your care. Make sure the new water is the same temperature and that you remove the chlorine with products your client should have on hand.

Marine/saltwater aquariums require even more care than freshwater aquariums, so your client should provide you with very specific directions on how to care for the aquarium. If fish really interest you, you might think about getting your own aquarium and becoming experienced in its care. You can visit many websites on fish care, such as www.fishtankworld.com, or read a fish/aquarium magazine such as *Tropical Fish Hobbyist* magazine (for a subscription visit https://www.tfhmagazine.com.

If, however, you are not comfortable taking care of an aquarium and changing the water while making sure the temperature level is correct, let it be known on your website and brochures that you only do short-term feeding visits with fish. Some people have exotic fish in plush aquariums, and you may not want to get in "too deep," so to speak.

Ferrets

Ferrets have become common pets and are interesting animals. They are friendly and fun loving. They also bite, so wear gloves. They have a few peculiarities that you should know about.

Ferrets are meat eaters. Their digestive systems work quickly, and because vegetable matter takes longer to digest, ferrets cannot get what they need from a strict vegetarian diet. Ferrets can be fussy eaters, and ultimately, they don't eat much, so many owners buy high-quality food (sometimes cat food) for their ferrets.

Some pet ferrets are allowed the run of the house and have been trained to wear a collar; many owners put a bell on their ferret so they know where it is. While under your care, pet ferrets may be confined to a room or cage, but they will appreciate some kicking around time.

If other pets live in the household—dogs and cats, especially—be sure to know how the animals get along and if it is OK for them to roam the house together while you are there.

According to Ferret Central, ferrets are often given hair ball remedies similar to the ones given to cats. Not only do ferrets have problems with hair balls, but they also often eat rubber bands and other small items found around the house. The hair ball remedy helps them pass those items through their system.

Ferrets are often also trained to use litter boxes. You should know from the owner what kind of litter they use and what kind the pet prefers. Some brands of litters that are used for cats are not recommended for ferrets because of differences in elimination habits, while other brands are fine.

Ferrets are very entertaining and inquisitive animals. Although you probably will not be hired just to care for a couple of ferrets, you may find them an enjoyable addition to your repertoire as a pet-sitter.

Rabbits

As another pet favorite among children, rabbits are more often housed inside than perhaps in the past when they were relegated to a small cage in the backyard. Rabbit owners often let their rabbits out for supervised runs around the house on a daily basis. And yes, rabbits chew on electrical cords, speaker wires, and other things that either are either dangerous or a pain to replace or repair. Some rabbit owners have portable pens in their yards for their rabbits to get some fresh air, sunshine, and a little grass. The most dedicated of rabbit owners build elaborate outdoor pens for their pets to have extended outside run-around time. While in your care, however, be sure these excursions are well-supervised because rabbits dig, their predators also dig, and portable cages can be easily overturned.

Unfortunately, rabbits seem rather delicate when it comes to health and care. The other thing that frequently happens is their owners become disinterested after the initial enthusiasm—especially when the rabbit is obtained as a little bunny and probably as a gift—and, therefore, you may find that rabbit care is often an afterthought. Also, many rabbits do not stay in the household more than a few months before they die, are given away, are given up to a shelter, or unfortunately are set free (this is not a good thing for a domesticated rabbit; it will not last long, succumbing either to predators or to an inability to care for itself).

tip

According to the *Clinical Textbook for Veterinary Technicians*, the proper way to restrain a ferret is to hold it by the scruff of the neck. You need to support its lower body with the other hand if you have someone else who can examine the animal, or with your lap if you need to examine the animal yourself. The book also says that sometimes this technique causes the ferret to gap its mouth open in a yawn, making it easy to examine the mouth, which can be helpful if you are trying to determine if the ferret has something stuck in its mouth or throat.

Reptiles

You may never have expected to care for a reptile, but more than several million reptiles are kept as pets in the U.S., so there's a good chance you may run across one or two in

► Use Caution With Children

You should never bring anyone with you on your pet-care visits. People are entrusting you to come into their homes and nobody else. Bringing children with you is an especially bad idea as the pets and the children may be frightened of each other. This can be a recipe for disaster and destroy your reputation with your client. If, however, you think there may be a few times in which you have no choice, let the client know in advance that this might happen once in a while. Then have a meet and greet where you have your child with you to meet the animal before your first pet-sitting or dog-walking appointment. If it's OK with the owner, you can do it, but lay out ground rules for your child before you enter the house, like "don't touch anything."

your pet-sitting business. Some common reptiles that veterinarians see as pets, according to the *Clinical Textbook for Veterinary Technicians,* Saunders, 9th Edition, 2017, are boa constrictors, pythons, and corn snakes (to name just a few possible pet snakes); different kinds of turtles; and lizards such as bearded dragons, iguanas, chameleons, and various types of geckos.

Reptile owners often do not hire pet-sitters just for a snake. You're more likely to care for a reptile in the form of adjunct care to a dog or cat. How do you want to handle these situations if a potential client calls? It is best to give an upfront "no" if you just can't picture yourself feeding a snake live mice (although most snake owners feed frozen mice, not live!).

You may want to know a little about snake capture and restraint in case Mr. Boa gets loose or you need to get him out of his cage. The owner should be able to teach you (in fact, insist on it). Owners should have tongs, a "snake hook," or a pole snare in their collection of snake care items that can capture a snake around the base of the head—although in the case of large, coiling snakes you also need to restrain the tail end!

As for turtles and tortoises, they are rather easy to handle. The owner will tell you what to feed them and when to turn the light on/off for their tank. You'll need to change the water (which should be around 80 to 82 degrees Fahrenheit) and scoop out and flush feces. If you'll be taking care of a turtle or tortoise for a week, you'll also need to know how to clean the tank and where to put the pet while doing so. Some people close the drain, put a little warm (not hot) water in, and let them frolic in the bathtub for a little while. Then you'll need to do a quick, but thorough, cleaning of the bathtub.

Your best source of information about reptile care is the pet owner. You need to follow the owner's instructions carefully to ensure the reptile stays stress-free while the owner is away.

The range of "familiar" household pets can be quite interesting with the various looks, sounds, and behaviors they exhibit. Each one needs its own type of care, and if you're going to take on the responsibilities for any one of these animals, you need to get a good understanding of the animal's needs.

tip

Lizards especially, but also other reptiles, need a full-spectrum light in their cage during the daytime.

In the next chapter we're heading out of the house and into the barn for some information on care for barnyard animals. This may be more challenging for city folks, but if you're moving to an area in which you will find farms, these animals can give you a whole different pet-care experience.

Barn-Animal Care

Not all pet-sitters will have barn animals on their list of pet-sitting options, especially if you're pet-sitting in places like San Francisco or Manhattan. But barn care can be lucrative if you are living in or near the right area.

Most people with barn animals will also have house pets (see also the section on barn cats at the end of this chapter), so these kinds of customers can take quite a lot of time and you can charge considerably more per visit than for just house-pet care.

In this chapter, we'll cover the big animals: horses, goats, sheep, and others you will likely encounter if you work in a barn.

Livestock Care

Don't solicit barn customers unless you have some experience with livestock. If you don't have experience but would like to get some, there are many ways you can learn. Like most things, if you offer your services for free, you can get all the experience you want. For instance, most large horse facilities are in a constant search for cheap help. They frequently exchange riding lessons or riding time for help cleaning stalls and other mundane chores.

If you are in an area where horse care can be one of your offerings, then you also should be able to find veterinarians who take care of large animals. Follow one of them around for a couple of days (with their permission, of course), and you will learn a lot about livestock care.

You probably won't find yourself being hired to sit for a large commercial facility, such as a dairy barn. To keep pet-sitting as your real business, you'll want to take on only livestock that are referred to as "backyard" animals—they may technically be livestock, but they are really considered pets by their owners.

tip

Keep a pair of boots in your vehicle that you wear only when you are at other people's barns. Also, always wash your hands before tending to your own animals. That way you can be more confident that you didn't bring home any organisms to your barn crew. You might also extend this courtesy to other people's barns—keep some Betadine® in a jug of water in your vehicle to rinse your boots before heading from a job at one barn to another. In fact, when barn-sitting or pet-sitting any animals, it's always a good idea to wash your hands before and after your visits.

Fees

Most pet-sitters who include barn care on their menu of services charge a general fee for a visit that includes care of one or two horses. Additional horses are charged per horse. So for instance, for $25 you provide a list of services for two horses for a morning visit.

For each additional horse, charge a surcharge of, say, $10 per horse. If they have other livestock, charge a fee that is fair compensation depending on the amount of work that is required to care for the animal(s). For example, if there is a pen of three sheep, you might charge an extra $10 to care for all the sheep but not $10 per sheep.

Another consideration in the colder climates is to charge extra for winter care because this requires additional time-consuming tasks, such as cracking ice out of buckets, taking blankets on and off horses, and maybe shoveling a path or two.

You should plan to spend at least an hour for a morning barn visit (see below for the kinds of tasks you need to do) and perhaps more depending on the number of animals. For an extended livestock-sitting job, you also need to make a late afternoon or evening visit, which should be shorter than the morning visit because you will probably need to clean stalls and paddocks only once a day. You may also be asked to come by in the middle of the day to feed some lunch.

Services

The services you provide for barn care may include:

- ▶ Feeding hay and grain
- ▶ Freshening water buckets
- ▶ Cleaning stalls
- ▶ Putting down fresh bedding
- ▶ Cleaning paddocks
- ▶ Light grooming
- ▶ Turning the horses out
- ▶ Putting on or removing blankets

Each individual client will have their own particular things to add to the list.

Horse clients can be good regular customers, hiring you to stop by each workday to feed some lunch hay, freshen water, and generally check on things.

These same clients may also hire you to be around when the horseshoe fitter (often also called a farrier or blacksmith) comes. Farriers typically prefer to have someone there who can hold the horse's lead rope while they remove shoes, trim feet, and nail on new shoes. This can take as little as 20 minutes for trimming the horse's hooves to as much as 45 minutes to an hour per horse, depending on the complication of the shoeing job.

tip

If you are doing lunchtime care for a horse-owning client who commutes to an office for a full-time job, you might occasionally be hired to hold the horse for the farrier (horseshoe fitter) or veterinarian. If you have another job, request that the owner make this appointment for a time near your typical lunch visit so you can combine the two visits.

Horse Care

Horses have delicate digestive systems that are not suited to their size and a domesticated lifestyle. Some special considerations for feeding horses are as follows:

tip

Aged horses (upper 20s and beyond) have sight and hearing loss just as older humans do. You need to be sure not to startle them, or you may get accidentally kicked!

- ▶ Horses need dust-free, mold-free, high-quality hay.
- ▶ To keep food moving through their digestive systems, horses drink ten to 15 gallons of water each day and need access to fresh, ice-free water at all times.
- ▶ Even though horses are large and need to eat between 10 to 20 percent of their body weight each day to maintain their weight, their stomachs are quite small and they need to take in their food in small increments.

Horse Vital Signs

Despite their reputation as high-strung animals, horses have low vital signs compared with most animals. Ranges are as follows:

- ▶ Temperature: Between 99 and 101 degrees Fahrenheit
- ▶ Pulse: Between 30 and 42 beats per minute
- ▶ Respiration: Between 8 and 16 breaths per minute

Bad Signs

The most common health concern you should look for when caring for horses is abdominal pain known as colic. Horses have a very simple digestive system, poorly designed for an animal their size. Any number of things can go wrong to cause a horse to develop abdominal pain. Trying to determine the cause of colic is important, but you definitely need to know how to recognize the signs of sickness. Some telltale signs that a colicky horse exhibits are as follows:

- ▶ *Disinterest in food.* If the horse has not finished their breakfast when you show up to feed dinner, this is a suspicious signal.
- ▶ *No manure in the stall.* Horses pass a lot of manure in a day, and if there isn't any present, the horse may be suffering from what is called *impaction colic*—a sort of mega case of constipation. The impaction itself has a cause, but the resulting abdominal pain is still known as colic.

▶ *Biting at their sides.* A horse in abdominal stress will frequently turn their head around and bite at their sides or kick at their belly because of the pain involved.

▶ *Profuse sweating and/or trembling.*

▶ *Getting up and down or rolling.* Rolling is to be avoided when a horse is suffering from colic. If the horse is affected, a large amount of food might be waiting in the stomach to pass through to the blocked intestine. This food causes the stomach to be heavy and can twist around when the horse rolls. Anyone who has taken care of horses knows that "walking the horse" is one of the most common suggestions for colic care, partly to help move the bowels, but also to keep the horse from rolling. But don't walk the stressed animal to exhaustion!

The key with any of these signs is to call the client's large-animal veterinarian immediately. The vet will ask about how the horse is acting, so report any observations you have. You should also know how to take vital signs so you can report them to the vet, especially the horse's temperature. Don't give pain medication until you get the OK from the vet; it can mask important tips for diagnosis.

Horse Handling

Be sure you are experienced in handling horses if you plan to add them to your pet-sitting list. However, even if you do have equine experience, get a quick lesson from the horse

▶ Weightlifting

A word of caution when it comes to barn work: lift with your knees. No kidding. A lot of things around a barn have the potential to require heavy lifting: full water buckets lifted to their hooks (tip: lift up a half-full bucket, then fill it with another half-full one); grain bags emptied into larger, mouseproof and horse-proof containers; bags of shavings; bales of hay; you name it.

While you can find many ways around this—water hoses that reach into stalls, hand trucks, tractors, etc.—many times backyard horse situations are not set up to be incredibly convenient. If you are dealing with one horse, it doesn't make much economic sense to spend a couple of thousand dollars to dig a trench and put in a closer water line.

If heavy lifting doesn't do much for you—or perhaps you even have back problems that require you to avoid heavy lifting at all costs—you may not want to get into barn-animal care at all. Even if you are able or don't mind lifting a bale of hay or bucket of water, you might want to require that the barn owner set things up as conveniently as possible for when you are visiting.

owner in how their horses are accustomed to being handled. Just because your horses are respectful when you feed or don't crowd you at the gate when you enter the corral doesn't mean other people's horses act the same way.

Never underestimate the strength of a half-ton animal, such as a horse. Even the gentlest of horses can accidentally hurt you. Many horses frighten easily, and as a prey animal, every single horse has self-preservation on the top of their list of concerns. The first instinctive move for a horse who feels like they need to protect themselves is to run—a horse who has been taught to respect humans shouldn't run you over, but in the heat of the moment, the horse may not even register that you are there, so stay out of the line of fire. The horse's second instinct, if they can't run, is to defend themselves by kicking with their hind legs, striking with their front legs, or, rarely, charging and baring their teeth.

Hand-feeding horses is never a good idea; even if you feed your own horses treats from your hand, don't do this with other people's horses. In fact, you need to learn from horse owners how they want their horses handled.

Horse Wounds

After learning what to do with a colic case, wound care is probably the main concern you will have with horse first aid. A rule of thumb is that the life-threatening seriousness of the wound is directly related to how close it is to the heart.

However, leg wounds can be of special concern because the rideability of a horse depends a lot on the condition of their legs. As with all animals, wounds first need to be thoroughly cleansed. Most wounds that do not require veterinary attention probably don't need to be wrapped; in fact, the horse probably won't keep the wrap on very long anyway. The two main types of wounds needing veterinary attention are:

1. Puncture wounds. These need to be thoroughly flushed and probably require a round of antibiotics.
2. Deep and long wounds. These will likely need to be stitched, although sometimes the ability to stitch the wound depends on where it is located.

Horses are also prone to eye trauma; these can often be self-healing, but it is not a bad idea to have a veterinarian check the eye for a scratched cornea or problems that could be permanent.

Feeding Horses

Horses typically like to eat grass, hay, haylage, fruit and vegetables, or concentrates like oats, barley, and corn. Ask the owner what they prefer to feed them and how much. Also make sure the horse has access to clean water. If the horse is kept in the stables, you'll likely be feeding the horse three times a day. The owner should have a feeding routine and feed the horse at regular intervals.

Note: Don't feed horses right before or after they exercise. As for exercise, the owner will tell you the horse's daily routine.

Sheep and Goats

Next to horses, sheep and goats are probably the most common barn animals you will encounter. Goats are often kept as companion animals for a single horse. Sheep are one of the few backyard farm animals who can be kept as pets but also offer a byproduct: wool. Both are fairly sturdy animals, and with attention to quality feed and rudimentary shelter (animal care is called *husbandry* in the livestock world), they thrive with minimal attention.

Goats, however, do demand attention. They are curious, entertaining, and sometimes frustrating animals! Contrary to popular belief, goats do not eat everything; however, they will *try* everything just to see if it suits their tastes. Most times it will not, and they move on. But once a goat lands on something that suits their discriminating taste buds, there is no stopping them. This can work in your favor when a loose goat needs to be lured back into a pen. Triscuit® crackers seem to be a favorite and have the added advantage of attracting the goat's attention with the crinkling inner wrapper. Goats also love apples, raisins, popcorn, and many other salty snacks. Some things are poisonous—including many landscaping shrubs, such as rhododendron and yew—but for the most part, unless starving, goats do not eat much that is bad for them.

The goat care you provide as a pet-sitter consists mostly of providing fresh water, hay, and maybe a little bit of grain, which is typically fed only to goats who are providing milk. If you sit for a milking doe, you will need to milk her twice a day as near to 12 hours apart as possible. If you've never milked a goat before, be sure to get a couple of lessons first!

Most goats are very friendly—too friendly in fact—but you occasionally run across the feisty goat who is interested in butting you. The barn owner will surely warn you about such an individual, but chances are goats of that nature are not kept long as pets. Most pet goats are *wethers*, which is the name for a neutered male goat or sheep.

Sheep are similar to goats, but they are often more timid. Sheep who have been heavily handled from lambs are quite tame and enjoy the company of people. But even these tamer sheep are often timid around strangers, so don't expect to sit around and cuddle with the sheep.

Sheep and goats are both ruminants—animals who have a four-part stomach that requires them to regurgitate what they have swallowed and pass it along to the next phase of digestion. The most common problem with ruminants (this group includes cows) is a blockage that doesn't allow them to burp (called *eructating* in polite company), thereby releasing the gas buildup that is caused by all the fermentation occurring in one of the animal's four stomachs. This problem is very serious and requires immediate veterinary attention.

Goat owners have been known to use the over-the-counter medication Gas-X° on mild cases of bloat, but often this only provides relief depending on the cause of the bloat.

In the summer months, goat- and sheep-sitting may require a little stall cleaning. However, in the winter months, many goat and sheep owners allow the stalls to build up with dropped hay (both sheep and goats are notorious hay wasters) to add to the warmth of the bedding.

Happy sheep and goats are eating, drinking, contentedly chewing their cuds, or walking around butting each other.

tip

Goats and sheep do not have top front teeth. That doesn't mean their bites don't hurt! You still need to be careful if you feed them by hand, and it is a good idea not to stick your fingers near or in their mouths. However, these animals do not tend to bite to be mean. Goats are curious animals, and one way they check things out is with their mouths. Proceed with caution— nothing is sacred, including your hair, your gloves, or that little tag on the back pocket of your jeans.

Cows

Most of the pet-sitting jobs you get in the barn will probably revolve around horses. However, horse owners may also own a cow or two. Some people with acreage raise their own meat animals; few people these days keep a family cow for milk.

Cows may be fed from a different source of hay than horses, so you need to be sure to learn exactly which haystack is meant to feed which animals. Neither the digestive nor the respiratory system of a cow is as sensitive as that of a horse, so cows are often fed lesser-quality hay. Although it won't hurt the cow to receive the horse's higher-quality hay, it does hurt the farmer's wallet. (There most definitely can be a negative effect on the horse if it is fed the lower-quality cow hay.) Cows are often fed fermented hay and grains called silage, which needs to be kept away from horses.

The biggest sign you want to watch for that indicates a potentially sick cow is one who is down and doesn't get up for long periods of time. So if you do your barn call in the evening and a cow is lying in a certain corner, and they are still there in the morning when you return, you probably need to call the large-animal veterinarian.

Pigs

Pigs in the barn represent quite a different situation than that of the potbellied house pets you'll read about in Chapter 11. Pigs, especially sows with young, can be quite aggressive, and most barns are set up so you feed and care for the pigs from outside the pen. For defense, pigs either run or bite, and they are equipped with substantial teeth to do so.

Be sure the barn owner leaves you detailed information about the pigs' care (there will probably be more than one). Pigs tend to eat prepared pelleted feed, and backyard pigs are often fed house scraps. Pigs eat a modest amount of hay, and like all animals, they need fresh water.

Pigs will have shelter and an area in which to roam. They also like to wallow in mud because they do not sweat, so mud keeps them cool in the summer. Pigs are normally very clean and tidy. They even tend to create a toilet area in their pen. They are quite smart.

Llamas and Alpacas

Both llamas and alpacas are members of the camelid genus. Farms with sheep often have a resident llama or two because they are very protective of the sheep flock. Llamas

▶ The Importance of Gates

The most critical thing you can do when it comes to giving good barn care is to check, double-check, recheck, and check once more just to be sure you have shut and latched gates. Many horse owners have things set up so you can feed and water the horse from outside the corral and you don't have to worry about gates. But if you are doing a longer-term barn-sitting job where you have to clean stalls and groom animals, you will be opening and closing gates.

The importance of good gate tending can't be underestimated. Wandering horses are a detriment to everyone—horses running in the streets can be hit by cars, seriously injuring and even killing both the horse and the occupants of the car. Loose horses can make their way to the grain room and kill themselves or cause irreversible illness by eating their way through a bag of grain.

Loose goats can decimate the neighbor's garden in a heartbeat. While they don't tend to move around as quickly as goats and horses, if sheep and cows are left loose long enough, they can cause lots of trouble as well as damage to property and themselves. Lock those gates and check them at least twice.

require very little care—they do need hay and fresh water, but they eat only a small amount each day.

Llamas do spit at things they consider a threat, including people, but the animal needs to be provoked or feel threatened to do this. So don't provoke the llama.

Alpacas are rather expensive creatures and are kept for their hair, which is used by hand spinners, weavers, knitters, and other fiber artists. Alpaca farmers will be sure to give you all the details you need to care for their valuable animals.

Other Types of Charges

You may find other animals in the mix at a backyard barn, but most fall under the categories discussed above. For instance, in the horse category, you may also encounter donkeys and mules, as well as a miniature of any of the equids: horse, donkey, or mule. Although Lilliputian in size, they all end up requiring the same basic care because their digestive systems work the same way.

A Word about Barn Cats

Barn care may include tending to the resident barn cats. In warmer weather or temperate climates, this may entail nothing more than making sure the cat dish is full of dry food. In cold climates, always be sure the barn cats have access to water; barn cats get savvy to the fact that they get a dish of warm water at each feeding of the livestock and show up to drink their fill before the water freezes.

Many times, the local stray population is the source for the barn's cats. Many of these strays get quite tame with the people they are accustomed to seeing every day. However, as a relative stranger, you may never see the barn cats when you visit.

If you do, you should be careful not to get too friendly with them. Because of their typical stray status, many barn cats may not be vaccinated simply because they can be difficult to catch!

Make sure the owner tells you what's what with the cats in the barn. You also need to know what their feelings are about veterinary care for the barn cats. If you do find that a resident barn cat seems ill, you can attempt to lure it into a crate and tote it off to the veterinarian, but the chances are slim that you can do that—or even that you will ever see the barn cat, especially if it is sick.

Caring for barn animals is a far cry from caring for domestic pets like dogs and cats. Many are larger and heavier, plus they have their own needs, their own food choices, and their own issues. Make sure you learn not only general information about the various animals you will be caring for but also some specifics that only the owner can fill you in on. Take notes because there may be a number of animals on the farm for which you will be responsible. It also helps to keep yourself in good physical shape because some of the larger animals, like horses, can tire you out.

In the next chapter we take a look at some of the less familiar pets people keep today. You might not encounter any of these, but it's worthwhile for you to have some handy information at the ready just in case.

Jungle Fever

Dogs and cats are the most common pets you will be hired to care for. However, people keep a huge range of animals as pets these days. Sometimes, your dog and cat clients also have other pets that come as part of the package, so it doesn't hurt to decide ahead of time what you will do if these animals come up when a new client calls. If you decide you will take on exotic animals, you'll need to know a little bit about them.

We'll talk about some of the more exotic pets you may come across, but first you need to consider one more thing: wild animals.

In most states, it is illegal to keep a "wild" animal as a pet unless you have been licensed by the state to do so. Wild animals include raccoons, skunks, foxes, and even wild species of fowl, such as ducks and geese.

Most states have several wild-animal rehabilitation facilities where people can bring animals they find injured or seemingly abandoned.

tip

Most young animals that "seem" abandoned are not at all; their mother or father is simply hunting or lurking nearby. Wild animals should be determined to be abandoned only if their parent is seen dead.

If you are asked to care for a wild animal as part of your pet-sitting responsibilities, it is best to say no. If the people are licensed to care for such an animal, they would not ask you to take care of the animal anyway, as they would want the care provided by an experienced wildlife person.

Chinchillas

Chinchillas have been the subject of various fads, so you may run across them from time to time. They have some idiosyncrasies that are worth noting.

First of all, chinchillas have sensitive digestive systems. They are typically fed pellets made especially for chinchillas. High-quality alfalfa or timothy hay is also an important part of their diet. It is recommended that chinchillas be given bottled water as they are very sensitive to giardia, a common parasite in water.

You pick up chinchillas by the base of their tails because they have a startling defense mechanism of slipping out of their fur! (It grows back.) They enjoy being rubbed and

▶ Illegal Eagles

Some exotics are illegal, such as any animal on the endangered species list. This does not come up very often, so you don't need to familiarize yourself with every single possible exotic pet that may be lurking in people's homes, but when you do come across something unfamiliar to you, do a little checking. This doesn't mean you have to turn your client in—that is up to you—but you certainly do not want to agree to take care of an animal that is illegal to own.

scratched around the head. Because their fur is full of lanolin, chinchillas also require a regular dust bath; pet stores actually sell something called *chinchilla dust*, which you put in a container and let the chinchilla roll around in.

Chinchillas are nocturnal. They like an ambient temperature of between 65 and 75 degrees Fahrenheit, and with excellent care, they can live from 15 to 30 years! Check out https://www.chinchillacity.com/chinchilla-information.html for information and/or Google other chinchilla sites.

Sugar Gliders

These unusual pets are popular among a small number of people. Sugar gliders resemble small flying squirrels, require quite a lot of attention and care, and do best in groups. Because they require lots of attention and companionship and develop strong bonds with their owners, many sugar-glider owners may never have pet-sitters care for their animals.

Sugar gliders urinate everywhere, so their cages need constant cleaning. Their food needs are very specific; you will need to get detailed instructions from the owner and be sure everything you need is in the house. Sugar gliders do bite if handled, but reportedly not hard enough to break the skin.

If you run across a sugar glider in your client list, check out the website www.thepetglider.com for information.

Hedgehogs

These days, hedgehogs are fairly popular. As with most exotics, pet stores carry food specifically for hedgehogs. Obesity is an issue with these spiny little creatures, so it's important they are not overfed.

To pick up a hedgehog, scoop it up from the side so you are picking it up by its soft underbelly. Hedgehogs curl up in a ball as a defense mechanism, but you can coax them out by rubbing their back spines in a circular motion.

▶ Pet Insurance

Although more likely to be taken out on dogs and cats, owners can get pet health insurance on exotics as well. Be sure to have a question on your client profile sheet that asks whether the client has pet insurance on their pet(s).

Hedgehogs need their cages cleaned about once a week. The animals are neat and can be trained to use a litter box in one corner of the cage. Their food and water containers should be cleaned and disinfected regularly, too. Like many small animals, hedgehogs like an ambient temperature of between 70 and 80 degrees Fahrenheit. Hedgehogs are susceptible to cancer, tumors, and something called *wobbly hedgehog syndrome*, which is exhibited by running laps in a cage or falling over.

Potbellied Pigs

Now we are bordering on farm animals. However, potbellied pigs are popular house pets and aren't really that exotic. They are typically friendly and clean and can even be housebroken. Their owners will tell you exactly how to care for them. And veterinarians are generally prepared to treat them as well; small-animal veterinary practices have seen more and more pet pigs over the years.

Pigs in general are difficult to handle, but potbellied pig pets are typically friendly and entertaining! If you are asked to sit for one, be sure it has been leash-trained and housebroken.

The most common complaint about pigs is that they are, well, pigs and are always on the hunt for food. This means you need to be careful about leaving food around and follow all the owner's instructions, which may include locking the refrigerator.

Also be sure any pet pig you sit for has been taught to respect humans. Pigs, like many animals, seek to be dominant and without appropriate training can become aggressive.

Being potbellied, there is nothing small about these animals—the type of pig kept as pets often reaches upward of 125 pounds!

Pet pigs need lots of exercise and stimulation, or they get bored and a bit unruly—a good reason many of them end up abandoned to shelters.

If you find you need to know more about potbellied pigs, check out the website of the North American Potbellied Pig Association (NAPPA) at https://petpigs.com.

Monkeys

What kid doesn't think that having a monkey as a pet would be just about the coolest thing? But as cool as it may seem, keeping monkeys as pets is not a responsibility to take lightly. A website from the University of Wisconsin (https://primate.wisc.edu) makes a prominent statement against keeping primates as pets, including the fact that they need very specific care and are able to transmit diseases to humans as well as contract diseases from humans, such as tuberculosis (TB) and herpes B.

If you do agree to tend to a primate, be sure the owner is conscientious. The monkey needs an annual physical and a TB vaccination, at least. Some states and localities require licenses to own an exotic pet like a monkey, especially species that can transmit human diseases.

The owners should let you know what they are providing the monkey for a nutritious diet. Commercially prepared foods are available. And yes, monkeys love bananas, but they need a diverse, balanced diet just like humans.

Monkeys need lots of exercise and entertainment, so free time is important. They also need a cage, and one that is secure enough to contain a monkey can be expensive. Many owners also put diapers on pet monkeys; otherwise, the house will get soiled.

Monkeys can be aggressive and dangerously so. If you choose to care for one in your pet-sitting responsibilities, it is probably best if the monkey can be left in their cage because they often bond with their human caretakers but are concerned about strangers.

Ultimately, monkeys are wild animals and probably are best left to the care of a person with experience caring for monkeys. If you Google "monkeys as pets" you will find some information on where you can have a monkey as a pet along with websites that will tell you it's a bad idea, for the owners and the monkeys. Having a monkey as a pet has been compared to having a toddler that never grows up. Proceed with caution.

▶ Internet Tip

When searching the internet, you'll usually get the most accurate information from well-known companies and popular animal organizations. This means sites such as Merck, the American Society for the Prevention of Cruelty to Animals (ASPCA), and other national animal-related organizations are the best places to look for highly reliable information.

However, that doesn't rule out other valuable sources, such as individual pet-owner sites and social media groups focused on one type of pet. You can gain a lot of information from these kinds of sites. You just need to keep in mind that the information can be full of technical errors—for example, giving the wrong name of a drug or general information about a particular animal based on one person's experience with their own pet.

Use all sources, but use them wisely. Always keep in mind that with pet-sitting, you are caring for someone else's pet, not your own, and you can't take chances. You need to make decisions with the specific pet owner in mind, not necessarily the way you would do things or people on social media would do things.

Wallabies

Unless you are pet-sitting in Australia, you probably won't run across a wallaby. But who knows! Like kangaroos, wallabies are a member of the marsupial family. They have pouches as well as large hind feet and legs like a kangaroo, but wallabies are miniature in scale compared with kangaroos. The largest of the species reach around two and a half feet tall and weigh around 50 pounds—comparable to a medium-size dog.

Most people who keep wallabies as pets have an outdoor cage—they do like to graze—and bring them in the house only when the owners are around and can pay attention to them. Wallabies are subject to stress-related illness and death, so as a pet-sitter, anything you can do to help them maintain their normal day is best. Wallabies are quite adaptable to temperature and weather changes, but like any outdoor animal, they need access to appropriate shelter from rain or cold wind.

Pet wallabies tend to be ones who were hand raised with a bottle, so they can be very friendly toward people.

Marketing Specialized Knowledge

After taking care of a few exotic pets, you may end up enjoying them for their unusualness. If you become knowledgeable enough, you could develop quite a specialty business.

However, as with any specialty, your service is needed by few customers within the general population. While you could have a thriving part-time pet-sitting business without leaving your high-intensity suburban development, to specialize in exotics, you need to cast your net considerably wider.

This means longer travel times to get to customers. It probably means providing longer visits as well. All of this means more gas for your vehicle and more time spent on one client, which all boils down to the fact that you must ask for higher fees to care for these pets.

To command higher fees, it is important to become very knowledgeable about the exotic pets you market yourself to care for. Find out which veterinarians in your area care for which exotic pets regularly. Bookmark the dozens of websites that discuss exotics. Also, keep in mind that your expertise in exotics is rare and that your clients should pay more for your knowledge. After all, you may be the only expert on rare birds in a 100-mile radius. Your clients need your services. Using your expertise in exotic and unique pets is one way to expand your business, which we will talk about in the next chapter. Keep in mind that you can charge more for additional travel time and your specialized expertise—but don't take advantage of the situation—the pet's health and well-being should override any thoughts of price gouging.

If your clients' animals are healthy and well-adjusted, then your clients themselves are one of your best sources of information. Imagine the cocktail party anecdotes you'll have!

Expanding Your Business

Your business can grow only so much by adding new clients. Once you add more clients than you can possibly handle yourself, you need to hire some help. Once you hire someone and add enough clients to keep you both busy, you'll need to hire another person, and so on. At some point in your business, you may want to expand your services instead of adding even more clients. Or maybe you will want to continue to add more clients but also expand your services.

Many possibilities for services you can provide exist. According to the American Pet Products Association, pet industry expenditures in 2019 topped $70 billion. Each year it seems pet owners are willing to spend more and more on their pets' health and well-being.

In this chapter we'll explore some of the ways in which you can grow your business.

Some Questions

You need to ask some key questions to determine whether to expand your business in a certain direction.

- ▶ What will an expansion cost in time?
- ▶ What will it cost in money?
- ▶ What will it bring to the business in terms of increased revenue?
- ▶ What will it bring to the business in terms of increased market range?
- ▶ How does it align with my mission and overall business goal(s)?

Each one of these questions needs to be considered in relation to the others.

Pet Specialist

One way you may get experience with other pets is when you have a client who has a pet iguana in addition to their dog and two cats that you care for. Or you might have a client who has a dog and a tank full of fish. Whether you choose to market your abilities with unusual pets is up to you, but it can be a sideline to your existing business. Word travels fast among owners of large snakes or exotics.

Expanding Revenue, Not Customers

Several ways to expand a business exist. One is obviously to market yourself to new clients. Another is to expand your reach. There is also the possibility of selling products, and in the service industry, you can expand your menu of services. Offering additional services and/ or new products are just a couple of possible ways to grow your revenue without increasing your customer base.

More Services

One way to get your existing customers to spend more money with your business is to offer more services than you currently provide. First, you need to look at your menu of services and figure out what you are not currently providing:

▶ Dog walking

▶ Grooming

▶ Taxi service to veterinary and grooming appointments

▶ Obedience training

▶ Show training

▶ Competition training

These are just a few of the possibilities.

The good news about most of that list, and about a lot of services, is that your business incurs little in the way of additional costs per service. Typically, the cost to you is in time and perhaps a few supplies. Your real costs are in obtaining your own education and then any additional equipment you need to provide the service.

Obviously, adding dog walking to your services doesn't cost anything in the way of supplies. Adding grooming takes both education on your part as well as some equipment expenditures, such as for clippers, a grooming table, some shampooing products, and a dryer.

The same goes for training, whether it's simple obedience or show and competitive training. Depending on how far into the industry you want to go, your expenditures can range from buying very few supplies to creating an agility course in your backyard.

All these options are additional services you can offer to your current customer base. It's not likely all your customers will want to avail themselves of your new services, but some will. And voila! You've expanded.

▶ Listen and Learn

What do your customers want? Do they talk about how difficult it is to get their cat's nails clipped? Are they pressed for time and can't get Fluffy to the vet when they know she needs to go? What are common areas in which your clients could use assistance? Hint: Usually it's about saving them time. People hiring pet-sitters usually have a reasonable amount of money, but like so many folks, they are pressed for time. How can you save them some time?

Products

The other way you can expand is to be a reseller of products that your existing customers might need. Many pet-related service providers find a product they really like and use on their own animals and then become a dealer for that product—certain kinds of leashes or collars, shampoo products, nutritional supplements, etc. This can be a great way to sell because your personal enthusiasm for the product comes across in a sincere way.

Or you may find that your customers use some everyday products you could sell. This makes your customers' lives a little easier and makes you some profit. You may consider selling nutritional supplements, over-the-counter products such as flea preparations, and even a brand of pet food.

A few disadvantages are associated with selling products, however:

▶ Products have an upfront cost associated with them. Many companies require their dealers to buy a certain quantity each month to keep their dealership status and to get the discount that you'll need to make a profit on the item.

▶ You need to have room to warehouse your supplies. With food, this warehousing can be very specific in terms of rodent-proofing.

▶ Pet owners are accustomed to having a huge array of choices when it comes to pet food, both dry and canned, as well as treats, leashes, dishes, and other paraphernalia. You may not have the space or inclination to satisfy the pet owner's need for this diversity.

▶ Anything you can think of is readily available online.

To sell products, you need to find a niche market or a way to personalize the product for the pet or pet owner. Perhaps you can provide a frame for one of the countless pet photos they have on their phone, offer to print photos, and have them framed.

One of the biggest markets for pet products are friends and family of the pet owner because they love giving pet-related gifts. Have a business card made up that mentions personalized gift items, then if the friend or neighbor calls, let them know what you can offer to do for them.

You can also consider selling products beyond your pet-sitting market area. You can market your products in fliers at local pet-related locales, like having a booth at a pet fair (or street fair). Any products you decide to carry don't have to be sold only to your pet-sitting customer base.

The product possibilities are endless. Ideas include handmade items such as leashes, collars, coats, dog and cat beds, blankets, biscuits, bowls, toys, kitty condos, and play areas.

Expanding On-Site

Perhaps instead of expanding your service business on the road, you would like to open a grooming shop where dog owners bring their dogs to you. This is a whole different business model, in which you will need the space and equipment to expand. If this is a homebased business, you might be setting up your business in the garage, provided you have proper ventilation and clearance from the zoning board and any tenant or condo association. One way to approach such expansion ideas is to determine what you would like to do, where you can do it, and how much you can charge.

Expansion Considerations

First, you need to decide how expansion can fit with your established pet-sitting business. Can you be around enough to have a grooming shop? Even an online store takes time to manage and make sure orders are fulfilled promptly. Or do you plan to hire someone to handle that aspect of the business for you? Hiring an experienced groomer can be the way to go— you don't have to pay to learn grooming yourself, and you can be ready to go as soon as the shop is ready. Plus, you can sell grooming-related products. The problem with bringing in an employee, such as a groomer, is that you are relying on this person to be reliable and do a great job. Adding staff also means a longer road to the revenue expansion you are looking for because that person will need to be paid, of course.

Also, while your residential area may be zoned for a type of business such as pet-sitting, which doesn't entail much in the way of traffic to your house, you may not be in a residential area zoned for having an actual on-premises grooming business. This means either taking your grooming business to your clients' homes or opening a shop somewhere else, which means paying rent or purchasing a commercial space, both of which do not come easily with the money in your change jar.

Not only does a commercial/retail space add expense to your business, but it comes with many other headaches,

tip

Always be sure to spend some time actually doing the kinds of services you are thinking of expanding into. To get some experience, work for a dog groomer, spend a few weeks as a clerk in a pet shop, and do whatever it takes to immerse yourself in the work long enough to get a sense of whether you would enjoy adding the task to your list of services. After all, you went into business for yourself so you could enjoy your work. You don't want to blow that whole concept by taking on something that drives you crazy!

including maintenance, cleaning, trash removal, and a bunch of little things you may not think of until you are swamped with a to-do list that has no relation to animals.

Thinking Outside the Box

Some unusual opportunities exist that relate to pet-sitting and can bring in additional revenue. Point your focus on less obvious ideas than walking or grooming and you might find a niche market to add to your existing business.

Office Care

Many doctors' waiting rooms, office visitor areas, and even restaurants have fish aquariums in their lobbies to soothe the waiting customer. If you become experienced in aquarium care, you could promote a service doing regular maintenance for office aquariums. You could take this one step further and create a business starting up aquariums for offices that don't currently have one. This could be all-inclusive—you could have a menu of offerings, including different-size tanks with a selection of fish you know how to care for and different prices for the type and number of fish they choose. Besides selling the tank and the fish, along with your maintenance contract, you could offer to keep the aquarium stocked with the same number of fish at all times. Aquarium care would probably require a weekly or even twice-weekly visit to the office, but like cleaning services, it could probably be done during off-hours and not interfere too much with your regular pet-sitting customers.

Night Watch or Off-Hour Feeding

Just because an animal hospital or pet shop is closed does not mean the animals don't need care. If you live in a populated enough area where several veterinary offices or pet shops are located, you may be able to make a whole business of off-hour service.

This service could involve being the regular off-hour caretaker certain days of the week. Or you could provide backup when the regular staff is sick or away.

Care probably includes feeding, cleaning cages, and perhaps providing a bit of exercise to the animals. It definitely includes checking on each animal and reporting to the appropriate person if any animal seems unwell.

Ecommerce

If you start a web business, be sure to advertise your site on all your pet-sitting literature, including your business cards.

The site should highlight all your product offerings and provide extensive information—with the internet, there's no reason to hold back on information. Show photos and tell sizes of anything that is size-specific. You should also, of course, make sure to promote your pet-sitting services by linking to the website you created for your pet-sitting business. Make sure to include some boundaries (literally). Even though your customer will pay shipping fees, overseas shipping can be more trouble than it's worth.

The pet-sitting website is mostly for advertising and information on your services. For your expansion to an ecommerce site, you'll need to accept credit card payments to be competitive and successful. You may also want to accept PayPal and even Venmo for small purchases.

A Bona Fide Kennel

One of the advantages of pet-sitting is that you go to the client's house, take care of the pets, and come home. End of story until the next visit. If you decide to take clients' pets to your home, you end up with a boarding kennel.

A potential headbutting concept here is that if you have a successful pet-sitting business, you have promoted the idea that pets are most comfortable in their own homes when their owners have to be away. So if you establish a kennel, you then have to make the case to your clients that your kennel is the best place to leave their pets.

You also need to take into consideration many factors, such as zoning laws, animal welfare legalities, and other things like vaccination laws that don't come into play as much when you are pet-sitting as you are not mixing a bunch of people's pets together.

Setting up a kennel in your home is likely to be more trouble than it's worth. You're better off finding an area zoned for such a business or buying an existing kennel from an established kennel owner looking to retire. Rather than expanding a pet-sitting business, this will probably replace it. You will be able to watch more animals at once, but you will also need enough boarders to cover rent and insurance costs.

tip

While web sales continue to climb, they are not free of complications. You need to be able to keep your site updated regularly if you want it to generate good business—nothing makes a potential customer less inclined to order from your site than if it was "last updated" two years ago.

Also make sure you stay abreast of popular items so you can stock up on what people want. And finally, provide a clear return policy and be very polite and helpful when it comes to customer service. And don't make promises you can't keep.

Doggie Day-Care Service

A new service that is becoming even more popular: doggie day care. Working dog owners are using doggie day-care facilities like never before. It's essentially multiple pet-sitting in one place of your choice.

These facilities are intended for a working dog owner to drop off their dog in the morning and pick up the dog at the end of the workday. For this to go smoothly, you need to consider a number of things:

► People tend to head to work and come home around the same time, so you need to be organized and have enough staff during key hours to help retrieve dogs and bring them to their owners in a timely manner. Most of your (human) clients are in a hurry to get to work, and they are eager to get home at the end of the day.

► You will need play areas and individual nap-time areas for the dogs. Actually, depending on the number of dogs you plan to take in at once, you'll probably need several play areas. Not all dogs get along, and you want to sort them into groups that play well together.

► The dogs need time to relax and take a break from playing with their buddies. These nap areas should have comfortable places to snooze, and they should be free from drafts and reasonably warm in winter and cool in summer. Make sure each area has its own water bowl.

► If you want to offer the best day care, you should have a covered or indoor play area so dogs can play in any weather.

► Lastly, the best doggie day-care facilities have enough staff to keep play areas well-supervised at all times. If you also offer grooming in your facility, perhaps you could design it so the grooming area overlooks the play area, with windows to the outdoors. Then while grooming, you can keep your eye on the play area. But you need to be able to drop what you are doing to immediately break up any fights or play that is too rough.

You can combine some product sales with your day-care facility. It makes a good combination to sell some of the more popular dog toys, treats, collars, leashes, and dog-care books.

Needless to say, this is not likely to be a business you will set up in your home. The liabilities, zoning laws, and so many other factors make it impractical unless you are only looking after two or three dogs. If you want to watch the herd, you'll need to rent space. Then the question you'll need to ask yourself is whether you can get enough regular clients to cover the costs of renting a space. Crunch the numbers carefully before moving forward; start out with three dogs at your house and see if you really want to branch out.

Memorial Services

Increased pet ownership means more pets who pass away. Owners are increasingly willing to pay for services such as private cremation for pets. Here are a few ideas of businesses you can consider for the person who has lost a beloved pet:

▶ *Sympathy cards.* A few are out there, but it is probably time for sympathy cards for pet loss to be a regular part of the card racks.

▶ *Urns.* Veterinarians often offer choices of cremated-remains receptacles that people can choose from. Why not make one of these choices a receptacle you make? If you are a woodworker, you can build wooden urns, or potters could make nice pottery ones. But if someone is going to bury the urn, they won't need to spend hundreds of dollars on a beautiful handcrafted urn that will be buried.

▶ *Plaques.* Engraved plaques with the pet's name and perhaps a quote or epigraph might be a side business to start.

▶ *Stones.* Like plaques, if an owner is going to bury their pet, there is a market for memorial stones—engraved and on a smaller scale than those seen in human cemeteries.

▶ *Cemetery/crematory.* These two options require property and adhering to strict regulations, but if you are ambitious, it is something to investigate.

▶ *Burial services.* Certainly, pet funerals happen now; who knows how long it will be before it becomes the norm? You might get ahead of the curve.

Franchises

In Chapter 2, you read a bit about franchises in general. This is an ever-increasing segment of the pet industry. A search on www.entrepreneur.com finds pet franchises not only in pet-sitting, but for gourmet treats, mobile pet grooming, waste removal, pet food delivery, pet photography, and even canine detection services. Starting your business by becoming a franchisee can be very rewarding, but you need to read up on franchises, know all the fees and costs in advance, and even talk with other franchise owners—if not in person, then on social media. Look for as much information as you can find on pet franchises in which you might be interested.

While franchises, as discussed, have their good and bad points, if you are looking to buy into a franchise for an expansion opportunity, you should be even more careful in your analysis and planning. For someone who has an established business, buying into a franchise business may mean giving up too much control. And the franchise may not allow you to have an unrelated pet business on the side. So go into the franchise world with your eyes wide open.

Classes

You may be able to expand your business at least a little by offering classes in pet care, pet first aid, basic obedience training, or other kinds of training. You'll need to find a space that allows classes with pets to be conducted.

Teaching can be a fun adjunct to your business, and it can bring in business as well! Plan your presentation in advance, practice, show your enthusiasm for pets as well as the subject you're teaching. Ask for questions, and if you don't know the answers, suggest places where they might find them (i.e., good websites or books on the topic). If people come up to talk with you after the class, that's a good sign; it means they liked what you had to say. Always have some business cards at the ready.

Training with or without the Pet Owner

Instead of giving classes, you can actually charge to train other people's dogs. This, of course, will mean learning how to train dogs and practicing your skills. You should probably first try training some dogs for your clients free of charge until you get the hang of it. Once you feel you are proficient, you can start charging modest fees with new clients to also help them train their dogs. You should include some one-on-one work with the owner and the dog together. You can give private lessons or run a class—but you'd better be good at it. If you develop a reputation for successfully training dogs, you can make good money. People will pay $30 to $80 per class for dog training, so it might be worthwhile to hone your skills.

Rehab

If you have nursing skills or any specialization (or want to get it) in physical therapy and other rehabilitation services for animals, you could promote it and find you gain a client or two a year. This can be lucrative because it requires specialized knowledge and a lot of care, but you need to know you can find customers who would pay for such a service. Talk with veterinarians about the need for such a service in your area. You may need to give this all you've got and include tools such as a heated pool for swim therapy. Although a pool is probably the most expensive equipment you would need, to be successful, to be taken seriously, and to get solid referrals from veterinarians, you need to have a seriously equipped rehab center in an area that is zoned for you to run this kind of business, along with the necessary licenses and insurance. If you do it right, you could have clients from a wide-ranging area.

Pet Taxi Service

Taxiing people's pets to and from veterinary appointments or grooming appointments can be an adjunct to your existing pet-sitting service. You can promote this service even to people who are not your sitting clients, although most pet-sitters who do this make it clear that existing clients and jobs come first.

Other Home-Related Services

As mentioned earlier, extra services over and above feeding, cleaning cat litter boxes, and letting dogs out can bring in extra money from additional fees and create more of an appeal for your services. They can also attract new customers. Pet owners hiring a pet-sitter are pleased to know that the same person is also willing to bring in the mail, water the plants, turn a few lights on or off, and generally help give the home the appearance of being occupied.

Some of these tasks may be things you do in the course of pet-sitting anyway; others may be above and beyond what you think is viable for services. Because you are at people's houses, and trusted, you may also become a house-sitter, which means adding on house-related jobs while staying in the owner's home. It does not mean throwing a party in their lovely home.

Get It in Writing

As you learned in Chapter 6, you will want to have a written contract with your clients. Even if they are repeat clients, you'll need to add on any new responsibilities, such as stopping by every weekday to let the dog out at midday, grooming, or training. Then renew the contract on a regular basis, perhaps every six months, or annually if nothing has changed. You can make seasonal contract renewals if what you need to do changes between winter and summer.

The contract should outline everything you are expected to do for the client. The core of the contract covers all the pet-related responsibilities, of course, as shown in the sample contract on pages 100 to 102. In an addendum at the end of the contract, add a list of anything else, such as the services mentioned in this chapter as add-ons that you and your client agree you will do.

Also, make it clear what expenses are covered in the contract and what are not. And in an age of endless texting, specify hours in which you can and cannot be contacted, and how to contact you. When house-sitting for a client, or working in another capacity, you don't need 50 texts (or emails or even phone calls, which are very rare these days).

> **tip**
>
> Always have your expansion services relate closely enough to your core business to make it logical to use your existing clients for marketing. Otherwise, you are starting a new business.

Extra Services

If you decide to add some home-care services or incorporate house-sitting into your pet-sitting business, you may be asked to do a number of tasks, from the obvious ones like getting the mail or watering the plants to some unexpected ones like having lunch with your client's mother-in-law or doing your client's son's science project. Only you can decide to what extent you will go in the way of additional services!

Plant Care

If you are willing to care for houseplants, the client should provide very specific instructions on how to do that—how many times to water the plants while the client is away, how much to water, whether to rotate the plants for location or the most sunlight.

This is not an "as you are walking up the driveway" kind of service. It not only requires special attention but the plants could die under your care! Be sure to follow instructions to a T, and be sure to have a clause in your contract that says you are not responsible for the plant's death. This is probably only a serious issue if the plant is a rare orchid that goes for $1,000 and has to be flown in from the Amazon on one particular day of the year, or if the pot is a one of a kind that the owner inherited from their great-grandmother and was made in the late-1800s, or if it's a different kind of pot that the client is now growing and selling legally.

Of course, if you accidentally knock a plant off a hanger, smash the pot, and mangle the plant, it would be good customer service to replace the plant (with a high-quality one from the florist—not a spindly one from the department store) and offer to replace or pay for the pot.

Cleaning

Again, housecleaning goes way beyond the scope of pet-sitting and other simple, as-you-go tasks. If you are inclined to take on this kind of work within the realm of house-sitting, it can fit into your business quite well. If the client is looking for daily cleaning, they probably should hire a dedicated house cleaner and not rely on the all-in-one pet- or house-sitter!

As a pet-sitter, you should plan to clean up any areas that are specifically related to the pets under your care. Litter boxes, food bowls, and water bowls should all be cleaned regularly and definitely on your last visit before the owner comes home. You should also plan to clean the areas around the litter box and food dishes. Shake pet blankets out and even wash them if they are washable, which may mean either hanging around long enough to wash and dry them or giving the dog a temporary replacement the next to last time you visit so you can take the blankets to wash at your home or a coin laundry. If anything gets soiled, be sure to give it special attention. If you are taking care of the pet in the owner's home, the owner should come home to a house that smells fresh and clean, and not like a kennel. That's not good for business.

If you've branched into house-sitting, you should get a list of specific rooms to be cleaned and instructions on what you need to do.

Shopping

Some owners might request you do shopping for them. This may be just shopping for pet food because the owners didn't get the chance to stock up before they left. Or they may actually ask if you would stock up on some basics and perishables for the clients right before they come home—items such as milk, juice, eggs, some meat and vegetables, or a prepared dish for a just-got-home dinner.

Whether you want to add this to your list of services is up for grabs.

If you agree to do this, ask the owner for an approximate amount of money upfront to cover the groceries. You shouldn't be using your money to cover these kinds of expenses. And charge a fee that would reasonably compensate you for your time and gas money. If any purchase requires a trip to some specialty shop, charge a surcharge. If you don't mind offering these services but don't want everyone to ask for them, surcharges help discourage all but those who would really find such a service helpful.

Dealing with Home-Maintenance Appointments

Many working homeowners have great difficulty scheduling maintenance appointments because it is hard to be there. This service is similar to pet-sitting and can either be an adjunct service to those clients who use you for their pet care or a separate service that you offer to the world at large.

So expand away to your heart's content if you need or want to. Just do it with your eyes open, and keep your ears tuned for innovative services to add to your core business.

And in the End

Hopefully you have learned a lot about what pet-sitters do and how they do it. For many people, whether they are sitting for domestic pets or barn animals, this is a short-term career choice on the way to pursuing other endeavors, some of which may include animals, others may not. For some with an entrepreneurial bent, pet-sitting can become a full-fledged business whereby you run a service with various pet-sitters working for you in one neighborhood, throughout a city, or even in multiple locations in several states.

Whatever you choose, enjoy the time you spend with animals. Pets, farm animals, or even more exotic animals can bring much joy in an otherwise stressful world. They are reminders of how simple life can be—eating, sleeping, playing, and simply being who they are. Whether they are your pets or the pets of your clients, you can make the most of sharing your time together and even learn from them.

As for the business, stay active, keep looking for ways to improve on what you offer, and try not to get too comfortable in a set routine or you may get bored. Remember to keep some cash on hand and do your bookkeeping chores on a regular basis. Also, because you're around pets all day, make time when you're at home to touch base with humans, like friends, family, and even other pet-sitters. Go beyond social media, emails, and texting—meet people in person or at least talk on the phone—yes, you can still talk on phones.

And finally, work shouldn't be a chore, so have fun—remember the old saying, "If you love what you do, you'll never work another day in your life."

Pet Business Resources

Hundreds of books have been written about dogs alone. For every animal you may care for, you can find dozens more books than those listed here. However, these are suggestions for a shelf of books you should have to help you with almost every situation that may arise.

You may find you prefer a different "owner's" veterinary manual than the ones listed here. Plan to spend some time reviewing the books online or in a local bookstore and choose the ones that work best for your needs. However, be sure to check the credibility of the author; you want to make sure the information is accurate.

Books about Animals

Aggression in Dogs, by Brenda Aloff, Dogwise Publishing, 2002.

Cat Owner's Home Veterinary Handbook, by Debra M. Eldredge, Delbert G. Carlson, Liisa D. Carlson, and James M. Giffin, Howell Book House, 3rd Edition, 2007.

Clinical Textbook for Veterinary Technicians, by Dennis M. McCurnin, DVM, MS, Dipl, and Joanna M. Bassert, VMD, Saunders, 2005.

Dog Owner's Home Veterinary Handbook, by Debra M. Eldredge, Liisa D. Carlson, Delbert G. Carlson, and James M. Giffin, Howell Book House, 2007.

Dr. Pitcairn's Complete Guide to Natural Health for Dogs and Cats, Richard H. Pitcairn and Susan Hubble Pitcairn, Rodale Books, 4th Edition, 2017.

Exotic Animal Medicine for the Veterinary Technician, by Bonnie Ballard, DVM, and Ryan Cheek, Wiley-Blackwell, 3rd Edition, 2016.

Horse Owner's Veterinary Handbook, by Thomas Gore, Paula Gore, and James M. Giffin, Howell Book House, 3rd Edition, 2008.

Keeping Livestock Healthy, by N. Bruce Haynes, DVM, Storey Publishing, 4th Edition, 2001.

Manual of Fish Health: Everything You Need to Know about Aquarium Fish, Their Environment, and Disease Prevention, by Chris Andrews, Adrian Exell, and Neville Carrington, Firefly Books, 2010.

Merck Veterinary Manual, by Susan E. Aiello and Michael A. Moses, Wiley, 11th Edition, 2016.

On Talking Terms with Dogs: Calming Signals, by Turid Rugaas, Dogwise Publishing, 2nd Edition, 2006.

Your Dog: The Owner's Manual: Hundreds of Secrets, Surprises, and Solutions for Raising a Happy, Healthy Dog, by Marty Becker, DVM, Grand Central Life and Style, 2011.

Books about Starting a Small Business

DIY Business Plan That Works: A Layman's Step by Step Guide to Creating Your Own Business Plan A to Z, by Robert R. Stimson, 2018.

The Everything Home-Based Business Book, by Jack Savage, Adams Media, 2000.

The Non-Obvious Guide to Small Business Marketing (without a Big Budget), by Rohit Bhargava, Ideapress Publishing, 2019.

Starting a Business QuickStart Guide: The Simplified Beginner's Guide to Launching a Successful Small Business, Turning Your Vision Into Reality, and Achieving Your Entrepreneurial Dream, by Ken Colwell, Ph.D., MBA, ClydeBank Media LLC, 2019.

Start Your Own Business: The Only Startup Book You'll Ever Need, by the Staff of Entrepreneur Media, Entrepreneur Press, 8th Edition, 2021.

Tax Savvy for Small Business: A Complete Tax Strategy Guide, by Frederick W. Daily, NOLO, 20th Edition, 2019.

Write Your Business Plan, by the Staff of Entrepreneur Media, Inc., Entrepreneur Press, 2015.

Websites

www.avma.org (American Veterinary Medical Association)

www.aspca.org

www.caninejournal.com

www.cathealth.com

www.chinchillacity.com

www.fishtankworld.com

www.petco.com

https://pethelpful.com

https://petpigs.com

http://petponder.com/?s=monkey

www.petsit.com

www.thepetglider.com

Places to Get Pet-Sitting Experience

www.care.com/pet-care

www.fetchpetcare.com

www.rover.com

https://wagwalking.com

Business Websites

www.allbusiness.com

www.bplans.com (excellent for business plans)

www.business.org

www.entrepreneur.com

www.gotprint.com (business cards)

www.irs.gov (everyone needs tax information)

www.moo.com (business cards)

www.sba.gov (Small Business Administration, excellent for business loan information)

https://smallbusiness.com

https://vistaprint.com

Website Building

GoDaddy, www.godaddy.com

Squarespace, www.squarespace.com

Wix, www.wix.com

Glossary

Animal husbandry: the caretaking of animals.

Better Business Bureau (BBB): a consumer watchdog organization that keeps tabs on businesses and their consumer relationships.

Bonding: a type of insurance protecting a homeowner from people who perform business services at their home.

Capillary refill time: how long it takes the mucous membranes to regain normal pink tones after blanching from pressure.

Colic: a stomach ache of any origin, and a common and serious ailment in horses.

Eructate: belching; in animal care usually referring to the important release of gases generated by ruminants such as cows, sheep, and goats that is generated as their feed breaks down in their digestive system.

Exotics: animals kept as pets who are a bit more unusual and often from "exotic" places.

Farrier: a person who works with iron who is also sometimes a horseshoer.

First aid: the immediate critical care given to a wounded or injured animal or person.

Independent contractors: people who work for themselves and contract their work out to a business; also called subcontractors.

Intramuscular: into the muscle, as in a method for administering an injected drug or vaccine.

Kennel: a facility where animals are taken care of for long periods, or an individual cage or crate used to contain an animal.

Pole snare: a type of restraint used to grab and restrain a snake (see also "snake hook").

Pulse: the number of heart beats per minute.

Rabies: a highly contagious and, when untreated, always fatal disease of the central nervous system in mammals.

Respiration: the number of breaths per minute.

Silage: a type of fermented feed usually fed to cows.

Snake hook: a type of restraint used to grab and restrain a snake (see also "pole snare").

Subcutaneous: under the skin, as in a method for administering an injected drug or vaccine.

Toxoplasmosis: a disease carried by parasites transferred in cat feces and damaging to an unborn fetus, making it important that pregnant women do not provide cat care.

Vaccines: drugs that help provide immunity to certain diseases.

Veterinary technician: a person who has graduated from a program that trains for technical services to veterinarians.

Vital signs: signs of life, such as pulse, respiration, and temperature.

Zoonosis: a disease that is transferable from animals to humans.

About the Author

Rich Mintzer is the author of more than 75 published non-fiction books, written or ghostwritten on a variety of topics, including many business titles. He also, edits, coaches writers, and teaches adult education classes on writing your first book. Rich resides in Westchester, New York, with his wife and two lovable cats, one that thinks he's a dog.

Index

Note: Page numbers for figures are in *italics* followed by the letter *f*.

A

accountants, 89–90

accounting, 86–89. *See also* financial management

accounting classes, 86

accounting software, 88

accrual method of accounting, 88. *See also* financial management

add-on services, 44, 45, 92, 140–141, 149–152

allergies to pets, 103

alpaca care, 127–128

ASPCA poison control center, 98

association memberships, 64

attorneys, 83

auto insurance, 64, 79

auto usage and expense records, 91

B

barn-animal care, 120–129

    about livestock care, 120

    barn cat care, 128–129

    cow care, 126

    donkey and mule care, 128

    fees for, 120–121

    gate tending, 127

    goat and sheep care, 125–126

    horse care, 120–125, 128

    llama and alpaca care, 127–128

    pig care, 127

    services in, 121

best in show competitions, 69–70

best practices for small businesses, 33–34

Better Business Bureau (BBB), 17, 73

bird care, 111–112

bites

   bird, 112

   cat, 102, 103

   dog, 76, 78, 80, 97, 102

   ferret, 114

   goat and sheep, 126

   known propensities to bite, 78

   pig, 127

   sugar glider, 133

bonding, 74, 77–78

bookkeeping, 86–89

brochures, 59–61

burnout, 33–34

business cards, 58–59

business plans, 22–24

business structures, 80

C

cages, cleaning, 43

capillary refill time (CRT), 101

cash accounting, 89. *See also* financial
   management

cat bites, 102, 103

cat care, 40, 42–43, 97, 99–105, 128–129

cat scratch disease, 102

cats, leash walking, 43

cell phones, 7

Certified Professional Pet Sitter (CPPS)
   credentials, 72

checking accounts, 87

chinchilla care, 132–133

cleaning pet areas, 43

client invoices and receipts, 91–92

client profile forms, 25–26, *27f–28f*, 105

client types, 46–48

colic in horses, 122–123

collections policies, 93–94

competitor research, 4–5

confidence, 6

confidentiality agreements, 81

contractors, 81–82

contracts, 76, 80, 99, 105, *106f–108f*, 149–
   150

corporations, 16

cow care, 126

CPPS (Certified Professional Pet Sitter)
   credentials, 72

credentials, 68–74

   BBB membership, 73

   best in show competition participation,
     69–70

   CPPS certification, 72

   dog training, 69

   experience with pets, 68–69

   first-aid training, 70–71

   grooming skills, 70

   nutrition expertise, 72–74

   PSI membership, 74

   references, 68

   resumes and, 74

   training from your veterinarian, 72

   veterinary technician credentials,
     71–72

CRT (capillary refill time), 101

customer service, 7–11

customers, finding, 46–48, 52–53

D

day care clients, 46

demographic service areas, 3–4

dental insurance, 79

differentiating yourself, 5

difficult clients, 9–11

disability insurance, 78

diseases transferable from animals to
   humans, 101, 102, 134–135

dog bites, 76, 78, 80, 97, 102. *See also* fighting
   dogs, breaking up

dog care
  cleaning pet areas, 43
  "doing business" outings, 40–42
  exercising, 42
  feeding, 96–98
  first aid, 99–101, 103–105
  illness, signs of, 103–104
  restraining dogs, 98–99
  toys, 98
  treats, 98
  vaccination requirements, 97
  vital signs, 99–101
  water, 40, 97–98
  wound care, 105
dog fights, breaking up, 78, 99. *See also* dog bites
dog training credentials, 69
doggie day-care services, 146–147
"doing business" outings, 40–42
donkey care, 128

E
eagles, illegal, 132
ecommerce sites, 144–145
email marketing, 55–57
emergency notification forms, 26, *31f–32f,* 105
employees, 80–84
employment-related taxes, 82–83
eructating, 126
exercising services, 42–43, 44
exotic pet care, 38, 131–137
expansion ideas, 140–152
  about expansion direction, 140
  about growth, 35
  boarding kennels, 145
  buying into a franchise, 16–18, 147–148
  doggie day-care services, 146–147
  extra home-related services, 149–152
  memorial services, 147

night watch services, 144
offering additional services/products, 44, 45, 92, 140–142
offering classes, 148
off-hour feeding services, 144
office care services, 144
pet taxi service, 149
rehabilitation services, 148–149
on-site expansion, 143–144
specialization in unusual pets, 140
starting an ecommerce site, 144–145
training dogs, 148

F
farriers, 121
feeding barn animals, 121–122, 124–127, 128
feeding birds, 112
feeding cats, 101
feeding dogs, 96–98
feeding fish, 113–114
feeding rodents, 113
feeding services, 39–40, 144
fees, setting, 33, 38, 44–46, 48–49, 110, 120–121, 136–137
ferret care, 114–115
fighting dogs, breaking up, 78, 99. *See also* dog bites
financial management, 85–94
  about, 85–86
  accounting methods, 88–89
  auto expenses, 91
  bookkeeping, 87–88
  checking accounts, 87
  client invoices and receipts, 91–92
  collections policies, 93–94
  financial policies, 93
  financial statements, 89
  fiscal years, 86–87
  paying yourself, 92, 94

payment options, 92–93

projections, 23

record keeping, 22, 87, 91–92

startup costs, 24–25, *25f*

taxes and, 16, 82–83, 86–87, 90–91

financial statements, 89

financing, 33, 34–35

first aid, dog and cat, 99–101, 103–105

first aid kits, 104

first aid training, 70–71

fiscal years, 86–87

fish care, 113–114

fliers, 52, 61

foods pets should not eat, 100

forms

    client profile forms, 25–26, *27f–28f*, 105

    emergency notification forms, 26, *31f–32f*, 105

    pet profile forms, 26, *29f–30f*, 105

    service contracts, 76, 80, 99, 105, *106f–108f*, 149–150

    startup expenses worksheet, 24–25

franchises, buying into, 16–18, 147–148

G

gate tending, 127

goal of pet-sitting services, 38

goat care, 125–126

grooming credentials, 70

grooming services, 43–44, 141

grooming shops, 143–144

growing your business. *See* expansion ideas

guinea pig care, 112–113

H

hamster care, 112–113

health insurance for pets, 98, 133

health insurance for you, 33, 78–79

heaving lifting cautions, 123

hedgehog care, 133–134

hiring employees, 34, 80–84

home-maintenance appointment services, 151–152

home-related services, 149–152

horse care, 120–125, 128

horseshoe fitters, 121

housecleaning services, 151

house-pet care, 110–117. *See also* cat care; dog care

    bird care, 111–112

    caring for additional animals, 110–111

    cleaning cages, 110

    exercise instructions, 110

    feeding instructions, 110

    ferret care, 114–115

    fish care, 113–114

    illness, signs of, 110

    rabbit care, 115

    reptile care, 115–116

    rodent care, 112–113

    saying "No" to caring for some types of animals, 111

husbandry, 125

I

illness, signs of

    about, 110

    cow, 126

    dog and cat, 103–105

    goat and sheep, 126

    horse, 122–123

independent contractors, 81–82

infectious diseases, 101, 102, 134–135

information packets, 53

in-home pet-sitting, 18–19

insurance, 33, 77–79, 82

insurance brokers, 79

K

kennel in your home, 145

L

lawyers, 83

legal issues, 80

liability insurance, 74, 77

licensed veterinary technicians (LVTs), 71–72

lifting, heavy, 123

limited partnerships, 16

livestock care. *See* barn-animal care

lizard care, 115–117

llama care, 127–128

loans, 33

long-weekender clients, 47

M

marketing, definition of, 52

marketing plans, 53–54

marketing strategies, 52–66. *See also* credentials

association membership as, 64

developing exotic and unique pet expertise, 136–137, 140

differentiating yourself, 5

email marketing, 55–57

finding customers, 52–53

fliers, 52, 61

implementing, 65–66

information packets, 53

marketing at pet-friendly hotels, 10

marketing to humans vs. to pets, 2

online marketing, 54–55

paid advertising, 61–62

press releases, 63

print materials, 57–61, 65–66

social media marketing, 57

speaking engagements, 65

vehicle signs, 63–64

memorial services, 147

Merck Veterinary Manual (Aiello & Moses), 111

monkey care, 134–135

mule care, 128

muzzles, 98–99

N

naming your business, 14

newsletters, 55–57

night watch services, 144

noncompete agreements, 81–82

nutrition expertise, 72–74

O

off-hour feeding services, 144

office care services, 144

online marketing, 54–55

on-site expansion, 143–144

operating capital, 34

orf virus, 102

P

paid advertising, 61–62

parakeet care, 111–112

partnerships, 16

paying yourself, 92, 94

payment options, 33, 92–93

pet care in your home, 19–20

pet health insurance, 98, 133

pet profile forms, 26, *29f–30f*, 105

Pet Sitters International (PSI) membership, 74

pet taxi service, 149

pet-sitting businesses

about, 2–3

advantages of, 49

competitor research, 4–5

demographic service areas, 3–4

differentiating yourself, 5

goal of, 38

reasons people need pet-sitters, 3–4

steps to starting, 2–3

traits and skills for success, 5–11

pet-sitting information sources, 135

pig care, 127

planning your business, 22–24

plant care services, 150–151

poison control centers, 98

potbellied pig care, 134

press releases, 63

print marketing materials, 57–61

products, selling, 142

professionalism, 7

PSI (Pet Sitters International) membership, 74

pulse, dog and cat, 100

R

rabbit care, 115

rabies, 102

rates, setting, 33, 38, 44–46, 48–49, 110, 120–121, 136–137

record keeping, 22, 87, 91–92

references, 68

rehabilitation services, 148–149

reliability, 5–6

reptile care, 115–116

respiration, dog and cat, 100–101

restraining cats, 101–103

restraining dogs, 98–99

resumes, 74

rodent care, 112–113

S

salary expectations, 48–49. *See also* fees, setting

service contracts, 76, 80, 99, 105, *106f–108f*, 149–150

services

about, 37

add-on, 44, 45, 92, 140–141, 149–152

cleaning pet areas, 43

client types and, 46–48

exercising, 42–43, 44

feeding, 39–40

goal of pet-sitting services, 38

grooming, 43–44, 70, 141

outings for doing business, 40–42

salary expectations for, 48–49

setting rates for, 33, 38, 44–46, 48–49, 110, 120–121, 136–137

sheep care, 125–126

shopping services, 151

side jobs as pet-sitter, 20–21

signs, 63–64, 65

slogans, 60

snake care, 115–116

social media marketing, 57

sole proprietorships, 14–16

speaking engagements, 65

startup costs, 24, *25f*

startup financing, 32–33

structuring your business, 14–16, 80

subcontractors, 81–82

sugar glider care, 133

T

Tax Guide for Small Business (IRS Publication 334), 90

taxes, 16, 82–83, 86–87, 90–91

taxi service to pet appointments, 149

teaching, 148

temperature, dog and cat, 99–100

toxoplasmosis, 101, 102

toys, dog, 98

training credentials, 69

training from your veterinarian, 72

training other people's dogs, 148

travel time, 38

traveling clients, 47–48

treats, dog, 98

trust, 6

turtle care, 115–116

V

vaccination requirements, dog and cat, 97
vehicle signs, 63–64
veterinary technician credentials, 71–72
vital signs, dog and cat, 99–101
vital signs, horse, 122

W

wallaby care, 136
water for barn animals, 121–122, 123, 125, 127–128
water for pets, 40, 97–98, 101, 112, 113
water in fish tanks, 113–114

water in turtle tanks, 116
websites, 54–55, 145
wild animal care, 131–137
workers' compensation insurance, 82
wound care, dog and cat, 105
wound care, horse, 124

Z

zoning ordinances, 21–22
zoonoses, 101, 102, 134–135

CPSIA information can be obtained
at www.ICGtesting.com
Printed in the USA
JSHW040208231022
31967JS00001B/1